LANGUAGE AND LITERACY S

Dorothy S. Strickland, FOUNDING EDI
Celia Genishi and Donna E. Alvermann, SERIES EDITORS

ADVISORY BOARD: Richard Allington, Kathryn Au, Bernice Cullinan, Colette Daiute, Anne Haas Dyson, Carole Edelsky, Janet Emig, Shirley Brice Heath, Connie Juel, Susan Lytle, Timothy Shanahan

---

* Volumes with an asterisk following the title are a part of the NCRLL set: Approaches to Language and Literacy Research, edited by JoBeth Allen and Donna E. Alvermann.

(Continued)

Children's Language

CONNECTING READING, WRITING, AND TALK

Judith Wells Lindfors

Foreword by Vivian Gussin Paley

Teachers College, Columbia University
New York and London

Published by Teachers College Press, 1234 Amsterdam Avenue, New York, NY
10027

Library of Congress Cataloging-in-Publication Data

Lindfors, Judith Wells.
    Children's language : connecting reading, writing, and talk / Judith Wells
Lindfors ; foreword by Vivian Gussin Paley.
        p. cm. — (Language and literacy series)
    Includes bibliographical references and index.
    ISBN 978-0-8077-4885-5 (pbk. : alk. paper) — ISBN 978-0-8077-4886-2
(hardcover : alk. paper)   1. Language arts (Elementary)   2. Children—
Language.   I. Title.
    LB1576.L533 2008
    372.6—dc22   2008007801

ISBN 978-0-8077-4885-5 (paper)
ISBN 978-0-8077-4886-2 (hardcover)

Printed on acid-free paper
Manufactured in the United States of America

15 14 13   8   7   6   5   4

To the SafePlace children
whose voices fill these pages

Contents

Foreword

Judith Wells Lindfors, a retired college professor, has a clear goal in mind. She wants the children at SafePlace to love books, to browse among them, to step inside them, memorize, and begin to read them. These are not unusual desires for a reading teacher, but the children Mrs. Lindfors teaches live in a domestic violence shelter and will probably be with her for only 3 to 8 weeks. Learning to love books would not seem to be a high priority—unless you are "Miss Judy."

Twice a week, Mrs. Lindfors wheels her book cart into the kindergarten and 1st-grade classroom of the secured schoolhouse on premises, then invites the children, one at a time, into the library heaven she calls "The Book Place." On this magical stage, teacher and child together search for the authentic story that will connect the child to the book. And we are witness to the "miracle moment" when it happens.

Ricky, Maria, Alejandro, and all the others you will meet on these pages, own few, if any, books. But their pathway to the printed page proceeds in much the same way as that of the children I have known. That is to say, they all recognize a good story when they hear it and are prepared to follow plot and character wherever they take them, into play and conversation, or, when the time comes, into writing and reading. After all, the children are already experienced storytellers and conversationalists when they arrive at the school doors. She needs only to show them that the words on paper make the same sense as those they know.

Judith Wells Lindfors, whose widely used texts on early language acquisition have informed generations of college students, returns in this book to her own one-on-one collaboration with children. Now she can feel again "the mystery that is the child's mind." In so doing, she may sound more like a friend and confidant than a reading teacher or academic, but this is to be expected when books become a personal and intimate matter between people.

Listen to Alejandro's response to a picture of two young dinosaurs in a book he has chosen to read with Miss Judy. She wonders if the dinosaurs are fighting, but he reassures her, "(The big one) roughhouses with his little brother but he pretends he's little so he won't hurt him." In another picture, when told that the mother dinosaur is feeding the baby, he says, "She has a string of beads—a necklace for her little girl." Alejandro may be a roaring dinosaur when he plays, but he finds the words to express the tenderness he feels toward his siblings when he reads with his teacher. He will borrow this book again and again, for it contains his own story and he must learn to read the words.

"Children learn from where they are, not from where we are," the author tells us in this well-written and easily accessible blend of theory and practice. We are shown the places where the *child as speaker and thinker* merge with the *child as writer and reader*. It is an exciting human adventure and, as in life itself, its vitality is often illuminated in mysterious and unexpected ways.

The account of how even one child is brought forward into the language of books and journal writing, and of how one teacher gains the insight with which to guide that child further, is the ultimate teacher story. Judith Wells Lindfors *is* this teacher, but she is also a philosopher, researcher, and child advocate who reawakens our faith in the natural powers of self-expression and curiosity to draw the child to the printed page. She does this by telling us moving and unique stories, and we respond as the children are programmed to do: We want to step into every story and make it our own. Judith Wells Lindfors's newest book informs and educates us, but, above all, it inspires us all to become better teachers.

—Vivian Gussin Paley
Chicago, Illinois

Preface

As we watch young children—our own or those of friends or relatives—we see that the vast majority learn to talk effortlessly and successfully. Some immature pronunciations or structures linger a while, and some irregular forms take a while to get sorted out. But by and large, kindergarten children can ask us questions, tell us what they want or don't want, joke with us, complain about others' actions and justify their own, and tell us about their experiences. They communicate with us and with one another, and we with them. They lack complete mastery, to be sure, but they have made a strong start and are moving right along. And they have accomplished this without a specific curriculum, without sequenced objectives, without periodic standardized tests. They have accomplished this through the ongoing, day-to-day business of interacting with others in various social contexts.

We may wonder, then, if written language and oral language are both *language*—if they are simply different systems for expressing meaning—then why do children acquire the one expression system (oral: speaking and listening) so effortlessly and successfully; yet—despite our carefully designed, step-by-step instructional sequences—so often experience difficulty and sometimes failure in acquiring the second expressive system (written: reading and writing)? When the child learns the first system (oral means of expression), he is also learning the world that the spoken words represent, its categories and relations. This would seem to be far more challenging than learning a second expressive system (visual symbols) for the words and world that the child already knows. So why are there so many children who have difficulty learning to read and write, when they so easily accomplished the seemingly more challenging task of learning all about the world and also our ways of representing it in talk? And what does it mean to say that speech and writing are both *language*? What exactly is the relationship of oral and written language and, especially, the acquisition of the two? How is the child's acquisition of written language (reading and writing) continuous with her (earlier) acquisition of oral language (speaking and listening)?

I often pondered these questions during the 27 years I taught language acquisition and language arts methods courses at The University of Texas. Then, in 2001, after I had retired, I began doing volunteer work at the small charter school at SafePlace, Austin's Domestic Violence and Sexual Assault Survival Center. My work with emergent and early developmental readers/writers there has enabled me to address my questions; specifically, to identify some important continuities and connections between a young child's oral and written language acquisition.

The setting I work in is the Kozmetsky Charter School for the children living at SafePlace. The school is located in a very secure compound that also includes the shelter (where the children are living), the warehouse (for donations), and the daycare center. The school opened in the fall of 2001 and is comprised of two nongraded classrooms (K/1/2, and 3rd grade and up) and a small library, The Book Place, which I started a few months after the school opened. Two mornings a week, I work with the children in the younger class, the majority of whom are 5 and 6 years old (kindergarten/1st grade).

There are several features of this classroom that distinguish it from a nongraded classroom in a public school:

1. There are only a few students at any given time, typically five to ten.
2. The children attend for short periods of time (however long it takes for the family to arrange a violence-free living situation into which they can move). This varies, but a typical stay is about 5 or 6 weeks.
3. Because the stays are brief, the composition of the class is constantly changing. The community is not a stable one. Children come and go, sometimes with no warning (as, for example, when a housing option suddenly becomes available and must be seized immediately).
4. The children in the younger class do not take any high-stakes standardized tests.
5. The diversity is remarkable across ethnicity, nationality, economic situation, and handicapping conditions, reflecting the pervasiveness of domestic violence in our society. (Any child currently housed at the shelter qualifies to come to the school.)

This K/1/2 classroom is a literacy-rich environment. The children have many authentic engagements with books. Their teacher is an avid reader herself and infuses book interactions throughout the curriculum.

- There is a listening center with a wonderful collection of tapes and accompanying book sets where friends can listen and read along together.
- There is a flannel board where the children can retell familiar stories and create new ones.
- The teacher reads aloud to the children at least twice a day.
- The children read to one another every day after lunch.
- Reading infuses math and science activities.
- In the comfortable book corner, there is an inviting collection of books and a picture of each child in the class reading a favorite book.
- Several times a week, the children read to their "reading buddies" in the daycare classrooms down the hall.
- The teacher often takes the children into The Book Place after lunch for a half-hour of exploring, browsing, or reading aloud.
- The children participate regularly in a writing workshop (a modified version designed to accommodate the small and ever-shifting community).

Books are at the heart of this classroom, and it usually takes only a few weeks for the children who are new to books to become active participants in this literate community.

It is the children from this K/1/2 classroom who, every Tuesday and Thursday, share one or several books with me in a group read-aloud, then come with me one at a time to The Book Place for some literacy engagement (e.g., sitting on the couch reading books with me or sitting at a small table writing a book or a journal entry), and, at the end of the day, take with them the note I have written to each one about our shared experience of the day.

You might think that working with children in this setting would be depressing. After all, it is domestic violence that has brought the children and their caregivers to the shelter. Indeed, there are moments of sadness:

Maria (6 years old, 1st grade), Dawn (7 years old, 1st grade), and I are seated at a small table. Dawn is drawing a picture while Maria is reading me the book she has written: *All About Me.* She turns to one page and reads, "I don't like when my mom gets hurt." Dawn, still drawing, says quietly, "I don't like that either."

Five-year-old Evita (kindergarten) writes a letter to her father: "I wish you were not in jail." On one page of the book she has written, *I Can Do All Kinds of Things,* she directs my attention to the tear she has drawn on the face of the little girl in her picture. Her text reads, "I don't like being alone."

And the children's eagerness for hugs suggests neediness as well as affection. Yet when I walk into the children's classroom or into the cafeteria while they are eating breakfast, I do not see "needy, traumatized children." What I see are *kids*—bright, funny, frustrating, unpredictable, challenging—all the things that children in any classroom might be.

During my first 5 years at SafePlace, I kept an informal, reflective journal as I tried to make sense of the experience I was having. I did not have a specific focus as I wrote, but simply recorded my spontaneous reactions to my Tuesday/Thursday encounters with the children. The journal includes descriptions, puzzlements, frustrations, reflections, plans, and wonderings, but most of all *stories* of what individual children said and did as we read and wrote together. The possibility of writing this book did not occur to me until well into my 4th year. I had never gone back and read my journal entries, but during that 4th year, I found myself wondering whether there might be something of interest in the writing. So, I read carefully through the 3½ years of journal entries and realized that I might have material there that would help me address my questions about the continuance of language acquisition processes as children learn to read and write. A closer study of the journal entries has enabled me to identify five continuities from oral into written language. These continuities are what this book is about.

You can see that my situation at SafePlace is unique. I have the opportunity to observe many individual children across a wide social spectrum as they engage with written language (reading texts, creating texts). I get to observe these children one at a time, up close and personal. How different this is from the classroom teacher's situation as she deals with 20-some children for 7 hours a day, 5 days a week (to say nothing of dealing with parents, administrators, test pressures, and so forth). It is precisely the uniqueness of my situation that has enabled me to learn what I pass on to you in this book. Whatever your role (teacher, parent, daycare professional), I hope that what I have learned will be helpful to you as you select, create, and structure reading and writing engagements for your group of developing readers and writers. I hope you will think about these literacy experiences from a language acquisition perspective, that is, a perspective that assumes that oral and written language development are similar and continuous in important ways.

In the coming pages, you'll see real children engaging in a variety of literacy activities: discussing books during read-aloud, reading predictable books, writing in reading response picture journals, writing letters to others, and making informal on-the-spot books (dictating, illustrating). You'll also encounter many more literacy activities that I mention in passing, such as shared reading of Big Books, browsing, reading to/with "buddies" from other classes, listening to favorite books at a listening center, and reading an adult's personal notes. If you are a teacher, you may want to adapt some of these for use in your own classroom. You'll also find the children engaging with a variety of books, and some of these, too, might find their way into your classroom—books for your read-alouds, for your library corner, for your shared reading events, for your reading/writing workshop minilessons, and so on. But although these classroom activities are very much present in this book, they are not its focus. The goal is to understand a deeper "activity"—namely, the child's continuing action of using the (oral) language competence he already has to master a second expression system: written language.

Acknowledgments

I am grateful to many people:

Katy Reeves of RSVP (Retirees and Seniors Volunteer Program). Thank you for identifying SafePlace as a good match for me, and for being supportive of my work there ever since.

The teachers lounge group at SafePlace: *Ms. Sherry (Kleinert), Ms. Vanessa (Jones), Ms. Katherine (Alt), Mr. Gabe (Rosales)*. Thank you for bringing such warmth and friendliness to my days at SafePlace.

Julia Spann, executive director of SafePlace. Thank you for being so supportive of this project from the moment when I first wandered into your office, manuscript in hand.

Barri Rosenbluth and *Tracy Alvarez*. Thank you for generously sharing your expertise with me in an interview that became the Appendix.

Grandma Beulah (Lemuel). Thank you for your strong, good-humored presence in the classroom and in the teachers lounge, where we share stories while the children are at recess.

And wonderful teacher *Ms. Marion (Parks)*. Thank you for sharing your children with me every Tuesday and Thursday.

"Kenny's" mother. Thank you for giving me permission to use "Kenny's" drawing and writing throughout this book, but especially in Chapter 5.

Mary Lou Serafine. Thank you for helping me think through the thorny legal challenges that were inevitable, given the sensitive setting of this work.

Becky King. Thank you for helping me keep on believing that kindergartens can be wonderful places for children, even in test-crazy Texas.

Jane Townsend. Thank you for reading and responding to earlier versions of this book and—especially—boosting my confidence in it.

Vivian Paley. Thank you for "listening" to the stories of SafePlace children that have filled my letters these past few years, and for responding to them so enthusiastically.

My editors at Teachers College Press: Series Editors *Celia Genishi,
  Dorothy Strickland,* and *Donna Alvermann,* and Acquisitions Editor
  Meg Lemke. Thank you for your enthusiasm for this project, and
  for your suggestions and continuing dialogue along the way.

Thanks to my family—supportive as always—but especially to *Ben,*
  who knew before I did that I would write this book.

Finally, thanks to my mother, Ruth Wells (who died in 2001) for
  advice she gave me when I was 9 years old. She found me sitting
  at the dining room table, struggling to write thank you notes to
  distant relatives I hardly knew, for Christmas gifts I didn't even
  like. "Oh, writing's not hard," she told me. "You imagine the
  person is right here, and then you just talk to them." It turned out
  to be good advice.

Author's Note

No name that I use in this book is the name of any child who has been in the 5-to-8-year-old classroom at the Kozmetsky School during the August-to-May school year, 2001 to 2006. Further, I do not know the surname of any child who has been in the school since its opening.

In some instances, I have modified details in order to ensure anonymity. I believe these changes will not affect the reader's understanding.

The children's literacy curriculum is carried out in the classroom, and my literacy interactions with the children are not a formal part of that. However, the classroom teacher and I work in a very close partnership, constantly sharing our observations and ideas about individual children.

I have alternated generic "he" and "she" by chapters: generic "he" in Chapters 1, 3, and 5; and generic "she" in Chapters 2, 4, and 6.

The children I work with are in a nongraded, K/1/2 classroom. However, they arrive at SafePlace with a grade designation and will return to a graded classroom when they leave. When I first mention a particular child, I give the child's age and grade if I have been able to retrieve this information from school records or from my journal. However, in some instances, this information is unavailable.

CHAPTER 1

Introduction

In this chapter, we begin by thinking about what language is, and then about the language ability that the kindergarten child brings to school. Three children (Jenna, Sarah, and Ricky) bring five "language continuities" into focus, that is, five aspects of language that are essential in the child's acquisition of speech (or sign language) and continue to be essential as the child learns to read and write. I describe the course of language development, and end the chapter by bringing you into a kindergarten classroom to listen to the teacher and children as they connect oral and written language.

WHAT IS LANGUAGE?

Ask a group of adults "What is language?" and you'll get as many different responses as there are individuals in the group. Some might focus on the social aspects of language: "Language is communication," or "Language is the expression of one's culture," or "Language defines a group as a community." Others might focus on the cognitive aspects of language: "Language is meaning—how we categorize and comprehend our world," or "Language is the basis of thought," or "Language is a system for relating meaning and expression, a system that is universal and innate." Those with a linguistic bent might say, "Language is a grammatical system for putting words together," or "Language is words and their meanings," or "Language is a system of sounds (or signs) we use when we speak." And for some, it would be aesthetic features that would define *language*: "Language is poetry and song," or "Language is voice—the expression of who we are."

And they would all be right.

Language is all these things and many more. It infuses our social, intellectual, linguistic, and aesthetic experience from birth. But it will always entail

expression of meaning to someone for some purpose.

Language invariably involves some manner of saying (overt expression), whether oral or written or signed. And we say something about something: meaning. We express content, substance, message. We don't babble; we convey.

- My grocery list is about what I need to buy.
- The letter is about Bob's getting laid off.
- The phone call is about what time the electrician is coming.
- The adult–infant conversation is about the teddy bear the infant is holding.
- The poem is about "the road not taken," about what life might have been.

Whatever the expression (the actual written or spoken or signed words put together in strings), it carries some meaning.

And we express this meaning to someone—a partner, a class, a reader, a group of friends, a sibling. For those of us who talk to ourselves or keep diaries or journals, we become the other, the "receiver" as well as the "sender," thus creating a dialogic structure for our own reflection.

And we are intentional in our languaging. Our purposes are many and diverse. We may be attempting to comfort, to deceive, to inform, to recall, to amuse, to inquire, to request, to persuade, to compliment, to invite . . . but we are always trying to do something with our words, to carry out some purpose.

THE KINDERGARTEN CHILD'S LANGUAGE COMPETENCE

The kindergartner comes to school with this experience of language. For 5 years, others have interacted with him, and with one another around him, expressing their various meanings for their various purposes. The child has been both an observer and a participant, using language as well as he can and also noticing how "experts" do it. He has been a kind of apprentice. He has gone a long way toward acquiring the expressive forms that his language community uses; toward making sense of the world in the ways that those around him do, sharing their concepts and the words they use to name them; toward achieving a variety of communication purposes. We are not surprised that most kindergartners put words together to inform, request, inquire, justify their actions, complain, invite, and so on. Maybe we should be surprised: This is an incredible achievement in a mere 5 years. Of course, the child's language mastery is not complete.

Overgeneralized forms (e.g., "comed," "goed," "runned," "brang") and immature pronunciations (e.g., "twuck" for "truck") and developmental structures ("Her did it") may still be present. Also, the child still has much to learn about the world, and as he does so, his language will grow to express his new understanding. Yet his knowledge of language is impressive. It is an understanding of language as an expressive system for conveying his meaning to others for various communication purposes.

In his 5 years of life, the child has encountered written language, too, another way of expressing meaning to various people for various purposes (see Figure 1.1). Many children will come to kindergarten with experience engaging with more extended written texts—picture books, fairy tales, nursery rhymes, information books, children's magazines. But virtually all kindergartners will have engaged with written language in a variety of contexts, and will have developed an impressive (though not total) mastery of oral language. All this experience has been language experience: people carrying out their communication purposes by expressing their meanings to one another.

How can someone who has been alive for only 5 years make such remarkable strides in mastering a system so complex that linguists spend their lives trying to figure out and describe its intricate workings? The child's grasp of language is, unlike the linguist's, quite unconscious for the most part. Ours is, too. Indeed, linguists use the term *native speaker intuition* to capture the speaker's sense of language, our recognition of what "sounds right" or is "appropriate" in a given situation. We know something sounds strange or rude or incorrect, though we might not be able to describe the problem. We use "simple" words such as *the* or *a* all the time, but would find it difficult to define them. (Have you ever looked up *the* in the dictionary?) Our knowledge of language, like the child's, is

Figure 1.1. Writing: Expression, Meaning, Interactants, Purpose

Expression	*Meaning*	*Interactants*	*Purpose*
"STOP" (sign)	don't go further	drivers	to request/command
"Nemo"	this is the video in this box	(potential) viewers	to inform
"Men"	this is the bathroom for males	people looking for a bathroom to use	to identify

more intuitive than it is conscious. But this intuitive, incredibly complex (from the linguist's point of view) oral communication system is what virtually every child in every linguistic community acquires. It's worth asking *how*, especially since the answer to this question has implications for the child's literacy development.

In the past several decades, a number of researchers have addressed this question: How does a child acquire language? Of course, there is still much to learn about this process, but there are a number of things we can now say with confidence about how a child from birth to age 5 acquires the language competence we see in the kindergarten child. Oral language is the child's first expressive system in these early years, so most of our findings relate to oral language development. But we are coming to understand more about the child's early and continuing acquisition of written language, too. We are now in a position to identify aspects of language acquisition—evident first in a child's oral language development—that continue to be basic to the child's acquisition of written language as well. If written language is language, then it should not surprise us to find continuities across the acquisition of the two different expression modes (oral and written).

CONTINUITIES FROM ORAL INTO WRITTEN LANGUAGE

Listen to two mothers in conversation with their infant daughters, Jenna (22 months), and Sarah (19 months).

It is Jenna's bedtime. Her mother is rocking her in Jenna's quiet, dimly lit bedroom.

Mother: So, Jenna, did you have a busy day today [at daycare]?

Jenna: paydo

Mother: Did you play with playdough today, Jenna?

Jenna: geen

Mother: You played with green playdough?

Jenna: Yeah. Marta [her daycare teacher].

Mother: Yes. You play with playdough with Marta.

Jenna: (points toward the door as if she wants to get to Marta and the playdough right now)

Mother: You'll play with playdough tomorrow. Now Marta is home sleeping. And Jenna is going to go to sleep, and Dylan [her brother] and Kelly [her sister] are going to go to sleep, and Mommy and Daddy are going to go to sleep.

Jenna: Marta seeping too. (Brenda Lindfors, personal communication)

Sarah is in the kitchen, eating lunch in her high chair, while her mother is working nearby.

Sarah: ha-hoooooo-he (spoken in a high, singsong voice)

Mother: (singing) "Hi ho, hi ho, it's off to work we go."

Sarah: (blowing attempt at whistling)

Mother: (whistles next line of song, then sings) "Hi ho"

Sarah: miomiomiowaaaaaa

Mother: (very dramatically) "Mirror, mirror on the wall, who's the fairest of them all?"

Sarah: owaa wiaawa mio*waa*miowa

Mother: (very dramatically) "Mirror, mirror on the wall," the wicked old queen says that in *Snow White*. "Mirror, mirror on the wall."

Sarah: eh-eh-eh-eh (falling intonation, stairstep fashion)

Mother: (witch voice) "Eh-eh-eh. Would you like an apple, deary?"

Sarah: ahba ("apple")

Mother: She takes an apple. Snow White takes an apple.

Sarah: uh-oh ("Uh-oh")

Mother: What happens when Snow White takes an apple? Then what happens? What happens with Snow White? She takes an apple and falls asleep forever.

Sarah: oh dis ("kiss")

Mother: Uh-hm. And then the prince comes and gives her a kiss. Yeah. And he comes on his white horse. (Lindfors, 1987, p. 207)

These children are becoming conversationalists; they are emergent conversationalists. Like all communication events, these conversations are purposeful: Jenna is informing her mother about what she did in daycare that day; Sarah is reliving a favorite story and bringing her mother into a shared ritual. These are real conversations, not drills or exercises. They are *authentic*: instances of purposeful social interaction.

Both the children and the mothers are thinking about what they are saying, not about how they are saying it. They are using particular sounds and sound combinations, words and word combinations, but their focus is on meaning—on playdough and Marta, on witches and poisoned apples. Theirs is a *meaning-orientation*.

Have you noticed the *collaboration* in these conversations? It is in partnership that these conversations are carried out. These two mothers create coherent conversations around their daughters' contributions. In collaboration with a more competent conversationalist, each child can go beyond herself. She can *be* the very thing she is *becoming*: a conversationalist. The collaboration makes this possible.

How have these children's language abilities developed to this degree? Jenna and Sarah certainly weren't able to converse like this at birth. But for a year and a half, others have interacted with them and with one another around them. Jenna and Sarah have been immersed in a sea of language that has provided literally millions of opportunities to observe how competent speakers use language and to engage in doing it themselves, however they are able to—through facial expression, gesture, word, word combinations. Some language acquisition researchers have called this process of observing and performing an *apprenticeship*: watching, noticing patterns in what more accomplished conversationalists do, and then doing it themselves.

These two conversations are one-time-only events: these individuals, this place, this moment, this shared experience. Even as a toddler, the child's expression is unique. Only Jenna would have had this particular conversation—these ideas expressed in these particular ways. Sarah is redoing a familiar script, but her rendering is her own—her selected details, her intonation, her laughter. *Individuality* is perhaps the single most distinctive (and amazing) fact of language from the beginning.

Here is another child: Ricky. He is 5 years old and just starting kindergarten. He comes to The Book Place with me. We sit on the couch and the first book we read is Sandra Boynton's *Blue Hat, Green Hat* (Boynton, 1995). On each page there are several outlined animal characters, each one wearing the same article of clothing (hats page, shirts page, shoes page, and so on). Only the clothing item is in color and beneath each character there are just two words: the name of the color and the name of the article of clothing (e.g., *blue hat, red shoes, yellow shirt*). Each clothing article gets a two-page spread, and for each, several characters are wearing the item properly, but one—a turkey—keeps getting it wrong (e.g., shoes on head, socks on hands), and each time the text under the turkey reads "*oops*." Finally, the turkey gets it right—is completely and correctly dressed from hat to shoes—and proceeds to dive into a swimming pool fully clad while the others, dressed in swimsuits, watch from the side. There is one final "*oops*" as the turkey dives into the pool.

> *JL:* Here's a book called *Blue Hat, Green Hat*. I'll read this book to you and then you can read it to me, OK? (reading) "Blue hat, green hat, red hat, oops!" (quietly) That's pretty silly. Wonder why he's putting that on wrong. (reading) "Red shirt, blue shirt, yellow shirt, oops!" (Ricky begins to smile.) (reading) "Yellow pants, red pants, green pants, oops!" (Ricky and I laugh.)

We continue reading and laughing our way through the rest of the book until the last page: "Yellow hat, green shirt, blue pants, purple socks, red shoes, Oops!"

Ricky takes the book from my hands and begins reading in a singsong voice, noticeably different from the "tune" of my reading.

> *Ricky:* Blue hat and green hat and red hat and oops. Red shirt and blue shirt and yellow shirt and oops.

He continues his singsongy reading to the end, closes the book, hugs it to his chest, and grins.

A week later, after I have read him *The Very Hungry Caterpillar* (Carle, 1987) several times, Ricky tells me, "Now I'll read it." He does.

> *Ricky:* The Big Hungry Caterpillar (cover)
> The Big Hungry Caterpillar (title page)
> One day one egg laid on a leaf.
> One day the uh the sun popped up.
> (inaudible)
> He ate the one apple.
> He ate the two plums. (Picture shows two pears.)
> And more plums. (Picture shows three plums.)
> He ate the um one two three four ate the four strawberries.
> He ate the five—one two three four five. He ate the five strawberries. (pause) What's this? (addressed to me)
> *JL:* Oranges.
> *Ricky:* Ate the five oranges.
> He ate one chocolate cake and one ice cream and one pickle one Swiss cheese, piece of salami, lollipop, one piece, one sausage one muffin and one slice of watermelon. And he was so sick.
> He ate the whole leaf and he finished it.
> He was so big he ate the whole leaf and he finished it. He went inside there (cocoon) for two days and he
> Turned into a butterfly! (From a tape transcription)

Ricky is an emergent reader. There are striking parallels between his behavior as an emergent reader and the behavior of Jenna and Sarah, the emergent conversationalists. Reading *Blue Hat, Green Hat* (Boynton, 1995) and *The Very Hungry Caterpillar* (Carle, 1987) is as purposeful for Ricky as the earlier conversations were for Jenna and Sarah. Both books delight Ricky and engage him. *Blue Hat* amuses him; *Caterpillar* tells a story. These are real purposes that real literature serves for us as adults. There is *authenticity* here. There are real reasons for Ricky to read these texts, just as there were real reasons for Jenna and Sarah to converse with their mothers.

And, like those early conversations, Ricky's reading is *meaning-oriented*. Ricky's meaning focus accounts for his laughing so hard at the turkey getting so mixed up (*Blue Hat*). He uses many of the words from the original text as he reads *Caterpillar* (one, two, popped, etc.), but often he uses his own words and/or phrasing, and when he does, his modification retains the meaning of the original.

As he reads *Caterpillar*, Ricky turns to me for assistance. "What's this?" he asks, pointing to the picture of five oranges. He accepts my help, but does not relinquish his control of the story (reading). My help is one aspect of the *collaboration* in this event. Ricky and I are partners here, but the text itself is another important partner. *Blue Hat, Green Hat* and *The Very Hungry Caterpillar* are enabling texts: They help Ricky *be* the very thing he is *becoming*—a reader. The format and the patterns in *Blue Hat* enable Ricky to predict what the text says. And *Caterpillar* offers support in its illustrations, in the counting, in the narrative story line. Ricky and I have read *Caterpillar* together several times, so his familiarity with this text supports his efforts also. With help—from adult and from text—Ricky moves forward.

You can see the *apprenticeship* at work in Ricky's reading of these texts. He has observed my reading; now he reads these texts himself, in his own way, but preserving the text meaning. His singsong, rhythmic reading of *Blue Hat* is quite different from my reading (the only reading of that text that he has heard), and his reading of the *Caterpillar* text is even more distinctive, not only in his word sequences, but also in the tunes present in his rendering—the ups and downs of his voice, his empathetic tone, his excitement. His *individuality*.

LANGUAGE ACQUISITION: A CONTINUOUS PROCESS

It is no coincidence that there are striking parallels between Jenna's and Sarah's conversations on the one hand, and Ricky's readings on the other. Oral language and written language are both language: systematic meaning-expression relationships. They develop in similar ways: Children discern and use patterns in the talk and print that they interact with and observe. To say that both expressive systems (oral and written) are language is to say (among other things) that both are communicatively purposeful and meaning-oriented, that both are learned through collaboration and apprenticeship, and that both are unique in each individual.

Over the past several decades, language acquisition researchers have documented the course of oral language development in many children from many countries acquiring many different languages. They have found that, though language acquisition differs in its specifics from child to child, it is strikingly similar in its general sequence and process for the vast majority of children, whatever the particular language they are learning. At first this might seem surprising. You might expect the learning of Chinese, Swahili, Vietnamese, and Zulu to look very different. But Chomskyean theory (Chomsky, 2000) helps to account for the striking similarities across languages. This theory asserts that every child is born with universal linguistic structures wired in the mind/brain. That is, every infant is born "knowing" what human language can be. Thus, children do not need to discover, for example, that one sentence can be embedded in another (e.g., I brought the book + you wanted the book = I brought the book you wanted) or that language has ways of expressing negation or possession or location or agent-object relations (e.g., The boy hit the ball), ways of "pointing" (here, there, this, that), and so on. An infant "knows" this already, and only needs to figure out how his particular language expresses these grammatical relationships. Roeper (2006) puts it this way: "Principles of grammar are inborn. . . . [A] child uses her innate knowledge of what human grammar must be like in the act of identifying the words and the special structures of [her] *particular* grammar" (p. 5, emphasis in original). And so it is not surprising to discover that sequences and processes of language acquisition are similar the world over, given that all infants are born with the same linguistic endowment (set of language possibilities), and they all perform basically the same task: figuring out how the language of their community expresses these basic structures and relationships.

Pattern plays a crucial role throughout the acquisition process. The world we live in—the way we perceive and categorize it—and the language we speak to represent it are patterned, not random, not chaotic. And human beings from birth are amazingly attentive to patterns. A patterned world and language and a pattern-finding and pattern-using child come together.

Two-month-old infants differentiate between persons and objects, responding quite differently to the two (Trevarthen, 1977). That is, they recognize one set of features being "person" and another set being "thing." Several months later, many infants go through a mother-versus-other stage, seeking their mother and withdrawing from strangers. At this point, the infant is differentiating among various humans, a more subtle distinction than the earlier person/object distinction. Clearly, patterns are at work here: This set of regularly recurring features is "mother," and this other set is "not-mother."

The infant's sensitivity to pattern is also evident early in her awareness of distinctive language sounds. One-month-olds, in carefully controlled laboratory research studies, have been found to distinguish between very similar sounds, such as /p/ and /b/ (Eimas et al., 1971). Researchers play a tape-recorded syllable /pa/ over and over again while the infant sucks on a pacifier. The child's sucking stabilizes. Then the researchers switch to /ba/ and there is a sudden burst of sucking. The sucking stabilizes again as /ba/ is repeated, and then the researchers switch back to /pa/ and again there is sudden agitation in the infant's sucking. The pattern in the infant's behavior is unmistakable: The syllable changes, the sucking changes.

Your turn–my turn is a pervasive interaction pattern, and it begins to develop early in the 1st year. When mothers interact with their infants, there is often a pattern of alternation: when one partner moves more, the other moves less, and then they reverse roles. Mother–infant vocalizations show this pattern also, with each partner vocalizing more when the other is more quiet. You can perhaps see why some have characterized this early turn-taking vocalization pattern as "proto-conversation." During the infant's 1st year, these turn-taking patterns become more complex sequences and routines, like peek-a-boo or give-and-take games.

These are but a few of many examples of the child attending to patterns during the 1st year: categories of objects and people and their labels, language sounds, turn-taking sequences. In short, the infant is tuning in to many different parts of that language system of expressing meaning to someone for some purpose. And from the outset, it's all about communication.

In the early months, children smile, gesture, cry, and vocalize. Adults often treat these nonverbal expressions as intentional, specific communication. The infant cries and Mother says, "He's hungry" or "His tummy hurts," as if the child has told her this in words. The child kicks his legs and waves his arms as the bottle comes into view and Mother says to the child, "Yes, you really want this bottle, don't you, little one?" The child reaches toward the bunny mobile overhead and Mother says, "Yes, that's a bunny, isn't it? Look at all those bunnies," as if the child's arm movement was intended to call Mother's attention to the mobile: "Look at that mobile." However unintentional the infant's body movements and sounds might be at first, over time they become intentional. It is as if the child is coaxed into intentionality by being treated as intentional. Pattern again: The child's specific gestures are responded to in the same ways, as conveying the same meanings, again and again. Patterned games continue, and soon peek-a-boo games and give-and-take games are accompanied by words—repeated scripts and routines. Later, some verbal scripts may come to stand on their own, without any support from action routines, as in the example of Sarah reliving the *Snow White* script.

By the end of the child's 1st year, words are likely to appear. *The* is the most frequently used word in the English language, but you will not find *the* among the child's first words. Frequency of use is not the issue; communicative power is the issue. The child's first words are those that do important communication work for him. Early words may include:

- social expressions such as *hi* and *bye-bye*
- labels of familiar people (*Mama*) or things (*doggie, ball, [ba]nana*)
- action words such as *go* and *fall*
- location words such as *down* and *here*
- describing words such as *hot* and *big*
- negatives such as *no*, and *allgone* (i.e., *it's not here*)
- words seeking repetition of something, such as *'gain* and *more*
- possessives such as *mine* (Lindfors, 1987)

These are communicatively powerful words. Not only are they substantive (unlike "grammatical nicety" words such as *the, does,* or *a*); they also can be used to initiate and carry on interaction. *Hi* and *bye-bye* invite the partner to respond. The child can use names of people, objects, actions, locations, and properties of objects to bring a partner to her focus of attention and, thus, start a conversation.

Child: (Holds up a toy.) Doggie.
Adult: Yes, that's your doggie, isn't it? What does the doggie say?

Child: (In high chair. Drops piece of hot dog.) Down.
Adult: Oops. It fell down. I'll pick it up. Better wash it.

Child: (Holds up a toy.) Doggie? (Single word spoken with rising intonation.)
Adult: Yes, it's a dog.

Negatives and possessives give the child ways to assert, to deny, to resist. *'Gain* and *more* enable the child to request the repetition of something he enjoys. Powerful words! Yet there is a sense that they are more than words. The child's single words in the one-word stage are sometimes called "one-word sentences." You can probably see why. The single word, spoken within the immediate context, has the import of a sentence: [It fell] *down*; [That is] *hot*; [It's] *allgone*; [I want] *more*; [That's] *mine*.

In the 2nd year, the child begins combining words, and now the implied relationships of the one-word stage are expressed more explicitly. As mother and child enter the house after playing in the park, the child might say "more bye-bye" (request), or comment "allgone outside" as mother closes the door. Standing in his crib, the child might drop the toy he is holding and say, "fall down." Pointing to his father's chair at the dining room table, he might say "daddy chair." When he can't get a toy to work the way he wants it to, he might hold it out to his mother and say, "Mommy fix." As he prepares to throw a ball to a partner, he may comment on the coming action: "Throw ball." Perhaps most useful of all is his question, "What dat?", a simple word combination that will enable him to elicit labels to add to his expanding vocabulary.

Notice that the child doesn't say "down fall" or "chair Daddy." He patterns his speech in the ways he has observed in the speech of others. As his experience increases, his vocabulary does, too: He learns new words to name his new understandings, but he also refines his words—categories and their labels—to more nearly match those of adults. Initially, *doggie* might be his word for dogs and cats and sheep; *chair* might refer to chairs and sofas and park benches. And, of course, over time, his sentences begin to include the "bits and pieces" as well as the heavy content words.

"Mommy go" becomes "Mommy going," and then "Mommy is going."
"Dat mine" becomes "That's mine."
"Daddy not come" becomes "Daddy didn't come."

One of the most dramatic examples of the young child's attentiveness to patterns is his early past tense and plural forms. It is his "mistakes" that indicate the process at work. The child overregularizes, using past-tense forms like "comed," "goed," "standed," and "brang," and plural forms like "mouses" and "mans." He has not heard others use these forms, so we know the child is not imitating, but rather is creating these forms by applying the regular patterns he has observed. Many young children sometimes imitate others, but overall, attentiveness to pattern overrides imitation as a description of the child's language acquisition process. Simple imitation can only account for children saying what they have heard others say. What is striking about the child's language from the beginning is that the child typically says what others do not say: "allgone outside," "more bye-bye," "Jenna runned," "my mouses." It is attentiveness to pattern that enables the child to construct novel utterances. He figures out the patterns and uses them to create his own communication.

During the preschool years, the child's oral language development continues, becoming

- *more complete:* for example, sentences include all the elements; various question forms occur; vocabulary increases
- *more complex:* for example, sentences include several related clauses; relationships such as cause-effect (Why?) and means-end (How?) are understood and expressed
- *more refined/precise:* for example, categories and their labels more closely match adults' categories and labels; hierarchical categories and labels (categories and subcategories) develop
- *more varied:* for example, more different purposes are expressed; a range of speaking styles develops as the child modifies his speech to different partners (talks differently to his doll and to his grandmother).

And at age 5, the child (Ricky perhaps) comes to kindergarten with this language experience behind him.

How will the course of Ricky's literacy acquisition continue through the next few years? This question is hard to answer, in part because we don't know what his formal instruction will be like. This is only one factor, of course, but it is a significant one. Although we may not know what lies ahead for Ricky, we know what language competence this emergent reader/writer brings to the classroom when we first meet him.

- We know that he has mastered oral language to an impressive degree. He knows what language is and how it works.
- We know from the way he approaches print that he expects it to be like oral language in some important ways: He engages with text authentically (laughing, empathizing); he orients toward meaning (creating "readings" that preserve the substance of familiar texts); he incorporates the support from "collaborators"— enabling adults and texts; he engages as an apprentice, observing

and performing; and he does all this in his own unique way—his response, his observations, his rendering. We hear his individual voice as he brings him-*self* into his interaction with text. In short, he comes to the page expecting to find language there.

- We know that he is attentive to patterns—that he notices them, figures them out, and constructs his own talk to fit them. We see this in his reading of *Blue Hat* and *Caterpillar*: his word combinations, his preservation of the narrative line, his use of familiar number sequences, his reliance on print/illustration matches, his observance of repetition.

This oral language competence enables Ricky to lead from strength as he begins to read and write, using what he knows already to learn something new.

In the coming pages, I present a language acquisition perspective. That is, I assume (1) that written language is, indeed, *language*; (2) that there are identifiable continuities across oral and written language in the kind of systems they are and in how children develop them; and (3) that we help children learn to read and write when we anchor our teaching practice in these continuities. The goal is that this perspective might help to inform the day-to-day decisions teachers make as they help children become readers and writers.

CONNECTING ORAL AND WRITTEN LANGUAGE

Continuities are important. So are connections. Vygotsky (1986) identified a kind of speech in 3- to 7-year-old children ("egocentric speech") that is related to their mental efforts, rather than to their attempts to communicate with others (their "social speech"). The child appears to be talking to himself as he carries out some tasks. Vygotsky's research indicated that ". . . egocentric speech . . . does not merely accompany the child's activity; it serves mental orientation . . . helps in overcoming difficulties; it is speech for oneself, intimately and usefully connected with the child's thinking" (Vygotsky, 1986, p. 228). It is speech that helps the child solve problems. In a well-known series of experiments, Vygotsky engaged young children in a variety of tasks and found that as the tasks became more difficult, the children's talk (egocentric speech) increased.

In the following examples from The Book Place, one senses that Alejandro's and Enrique's speech is directing their efforts as they create entries in their reading response journals:

Alejandro (6 years old, kindergarten) has just read *Brown Bear, Brown Bear* (Martin, 1995) and is now drawing a picture of a brown bear in his journal. He talks as he draws:

> A nose.
> Put a circle as his eyes.
> His body's brown.
> Big and huge big.
> He don't got no tail.

Enrique (5 years old, kindergarten) is drawing a brown bear, a red bird, and rain.

> I can do raining
> This is rain
> Rain coming

Then he makes a red border as he says,

> I color in red, red, red
> All of 'em red

There is a spontaneous talking/writing (drawing) connection in these individual events.

In classrooms, teachers often connect talk and writing in group events, too—events both formal and informal. Think of perfunctory print events—attendance slips, show-and-tell lists, names posted on cubbies, charts indicating classroom helpers—all instances of print that tends to get infused with talk. Think of early writing experiences—dictation, group writing events (such as when the teacher elicits the children's ideas about a shared experience—a fishing trip to the creek, a visit to the zoo—and writes these contributions on a sheet of newsprint that will be a page in the year-long class journal), or writing conferences with individual children as they work on a journal entry or a piece in writing workshop. In all these writing experiences, the children actually watch the magic as spoken words—*their* spoken words—become print.

These are but a few of the many typical examples of talk and writing connecting in mutually supportive ways in the classroom. Bringing the two together in the flow of classroom life may feel effortless, "natural." But the easy feel of bringing talk and writing together does not lessen the importance of doing so. The connection between the expressive system he has mastered and the expressive system he is learning is crucial for the child's literacy development.

Teachers' recognition of the importance of continuities from oral into written language, and of connections between oral and written language, informs excellent teaching in many classrooms, such as Marion Coffee's (Lindfors, 1994):

> The children are seated in a circle on the rug for Whole Group Study Time.
>
> *Marion:* Samantha is sad today. (The children look for Samantha in the circle and see a very unhappy classmate.)
>
> *Marion:* She's sad because she wanted to play in Big Blocks, but there were already six people so she couldn't. What could we say to Samantha to make her feel better? (Hands go up. Marion calls on a child.)
>
> *Child:* Samantha, you can play in Big Blocks tomorrow. (Samantha is still unhappily staring down at the rug.)
>
> *Marion:* She's still sad. What else can we tell her?
>
> *Child:* Samantha, you can play in Big Blocks first thing when you come in tomorrow. (No change in Samantha.)
>
> *Marion:* What could we do to be sure that Samantha gets to play in Big Blocks tomorrow?
>
> *Several children:* Write it down.
>
> *Marion:* OK. I'll write it right here on the chalkboard (behind her chair). (Sounding it out as she writes) "S-a-man-tha. B-ii-g Bl-o-ck-s". (Samantha is now watching Marion write on the chalkboard.)
>
> *Child:* But what if somebody erases it? Maybe you should write it up higher.
>
> *Child:* Yeah, but somebody could still stand up on a chair and erase it.
>
> *Marion:* Well, you know what I'll do? I'm going to do something I used to do last year and it worked. I'll write right here. (Sounding it out) "Do n-o-t e-ra-se."

A typical Circle Time event in this kindergarten. Typical and oh so powerful.

CHAPTER 2

Authenticity

Genuine communication purpose is the focus of this chapter. In it, you will meet many children who are creating and responding to texts that are and are not authentic. Ricky opens the chapter, and Maria ends it. In between, you'll find children responding to authentic and inauthentic literature, and writing (notes, copying, writing workshop) in ways that do or do not carry out real social purposes for them. And, once again, there are connections—between oral and written language, but also between the two sides of written language: reading and writing.

RICKY'S ENCOUNTER WITH INAUTHENTIC TEXT

You met Ricky in the last chapter, reading *Blue Hat, Green Hat* (Boynton, 1995) and *The Very Hungry Caterpillar* (Carle, 1987). A week after I had taped Ricky reading *Caterpillar*, he came to The Book Place carrying a book from home that he wanted to read with me, a pattern book called *Knock Knock* (Gref, 2002). He had not read this book before and no one had read it to him, but he had read other pattern books and knew that the procedure was to identify the pattern and then repeat it on every page, making minor adjustments according to the illustrations (e.g., I see a frog, I see a duck, I see a chicken). Ricky assumed that the pattern for this particular book was "I am a _____." It wasn't. Each page showed a dog character dressing up as a different animal and coming to a squirrel's home (presumably a friend). Each time, the dog names the animal he is pretending to be—"It is a *(animal's name)*,"—and the squirrel replies, "You look like a dog." Finally, the dog comes without a costume and he and the squirrel say in unison, "It is a dog." Ricky missed both the story line and the pattern entirely; he proceeded page after page with his "I am a _____." But what was particularly striking in his "reading" was his voice—his robot voice! It was a monotone, inanimate voice without rhythm, intonation, expression of any kind, and with a slight pause between words: I-am-a-dog-I-am-a-mouse-I-am-a-bunny. How could this be the same child who, a week before, had read

Caterpillar so expressively, so feelingly—his voice so tuneful, sympathetic, excited, tender? Where was the child who had read *Blue Hat* with such a lilting, swaying rhythm and lots of laughter and giggles? *Blue Hat*, after all, is a pattern book, too: On every page there are two words—color and clothing item—matching the pictures. The child only needs to figure out the pattern and apply it to the illustrations. But his reading of that book had been anything but robotic. He entered the *Blue Hat* text—his person, his s*elf* was there. But Ricky, the person, was absent from *Knock Knock*. Why?

Initially, *Blue Hat* and *Knock Knock* might seem very similar: On each page, there is a picture accompanied by patterned text. The difference is in the motivation that underlies the patterned text—the reason, the purpose for the pattern. The author's purpose in *Blue Hat* is aesthetic/literary; the author's purpose in *Knock Knock* is pedagogical. Boynton has crafted a work designed to amuse, delight, engage; the author of *Knock Knock* has crafted a text designed to teach a child to decode.

Ricky could not have told us, "*Blue Hat* is authentic (a text serving a real literary purpose) and *Knock Knock* is not," but his markedly different ways of engaging with the two texts indicates that they are different types of text for him. Each type calls for—and gets from Ricky—a different type of response.

RESPONDING TO AUTHENTIC (AND INAUTHENTIC) TEXTS

We read purposefully. Sometimes we read in order to gain information, solve a problem, or carry out an action. It's the way you might read a biology textbook, the instructions accompanying a new appliance, or a recipe for a dish you are preparing. Rosenblatt (1978) calls this an "efferent" orientation: "the reader's attention is focused primarily on what will remain . . . *after* the reading—the information to be acquired, the logical solution to a problem, the actions to be carried out" (p. 23). Other times we read for the experience of the moment. This is "aesthetic" reading, in which "the reader's primary concern is what happens *during* the actual reading event" (p. 24) and his attention "*is centered directly on what he is living through*" as he reads (p. 24). It is the way you might read an exciting mystery novel, a favorite poem, or a beautiful passage of scripture. This is the way Ricky engaged with *Blue Hat* and *Caterpillar*. He was not trying to learn about colors or caterpillars; he was living in the literary experience of the moment.

This efferent/aesthetic distinction has held up well over the years. No doubt it resonates for you as you think about your own reading. Sometimes you read for information *from* a text; sometimes you read for engagement *with* a text. Your *purpose* for reading influences your *way* of reading.

You can see that it is possible to read a particular text either aesthetically or efferently. For example, you might read a favorite Shakespeare sonnet aesthetically if you were reading it for pleasure, but you might read the same sonnet efferently if you were reading it as an assignment for a literature course (especially if you were preparing for an exam). But you can also see that some texts especially invite an aesthetic reading, while others especially invite an efferent reading. *Blue Hat* and *Caterpillar* invited—and got from Ricky—an aesthetic reading, not an efferent one (e.g., learning about caterpillars or colors). Ricky was oriented toward *engaging with the text*, not *learning from the text*.

What about *Knock Knock*? When Ricky read (his version of) this text, he did not read aesthetically (living a literary experience) or efferently (gaining some information to carry away). His purpose was apparently just to repeat what he believed to be the pattern on the pages. That his reading made no sense was not an issue for him. *Knock Knock* evoked neither a living-through orientation, nor a taking-away orientation. Ricky read this text in a robot voice, perhaps because he was reading a "robot text," a text without a pulse, a text that offered no literary invitation.

How different is children's engagement with authentic texts that invite them into aesthetic or efferent reading and response? Texts such as *Caterpillar* and *Tigress* (Dowson, 2004), for instance.

Tigress is a beautiful picture book that follows a mother tiger and her two cubs from the cubs' birth until they go off on their own as adults. There are two lines of text on each page, the first a narrative line following the cubs' first 2 years; the second, in italics, an expository line giving facts about tigers in general. When I read this book to the children for the first time, their response surprised me—the burst of chatter, observations, connections, comments, questions. It's the kind of engagement I don't expect on a first reading, but only after the book is more familiar. I wished that I had taped the discussion, to capture the lively conversation. So, 2 days later, I read this book again, this time with my tape recorder going. Listen now to four 6-year-old boys responding to this text:

> *JL:* Here's a book we've read before. The reason to do a book again is lots of times you think about things when you hear a book the second time that you didn't think about when you heard it the first time. So here comes *Tigress*. [Gestures toward the print on the first page, which is facing the children.] Remember this kind of book that has two

different lines? Here's how it goes. (I love the way this author begins
this book.) Gary, I see you have something to say before we start.

Gary: Tigers are very good at blending in.

JL: They are, and that's one of the first things it tells us. And it tells us that
by asking us a question. (Reading) "Twigs with whiskers? A tree with
a tail?" (Children laugh.) "Or is it a tigress, hiding? She can look exactly
like a patch of forest, just by being there. When she stalks slowly
through leaves and shadows, or crouches still in elephant grass, her
fiery, stripey coat seems to vanish like magic."

Chad: Read that one (pointing to the italicized expository line of text).

JL: OK. Here's the fact part. (reading) "Tigers are rarely seen, even
though they can grow as big as Shetland ponies." That's really big.

Gary: I didn't know that.

(Overlapping talk, including the question: What's a Shetland pony?)

JL: It's a kind of a horse. You know how big a horse is. (reading) "Tigers'
bright stripes are perfect camouflage in their natural surroundings."
'Cause they look like the elephant grass.

Kenny: I know that because um if I was in that tall grass nobody would see
me because I would be like this (he crouches down to demonstrate).

JL: You'd crouch down like that? That would be a way of hiding.

Wesley: Tigers would like to play hide and go seek. *(laughter)*

Gary: But it would be dangerous.

JL: Why?

Gary: 'Cause hiding in the grass inside the jungle.

Chad: No, because snakes could be under there.

Gary: Yeah. And tigers . . .

JL: (reading) "When the mothers hunt, the cubs are left unprotected.
Changing dens helps to fool predators, such as leopards and wild
dogs, that might kill the cubs."

Wesley: Wild dogs?

JL: Wild dogs. Those are very very fierce. You wouldn't want them to get
your baby cubs.

Wesley: What are wild dogs?

JL: Well, they're just what you would think. They're dogs, but they're a
special kind of dog that lives in the wild, not like the dogs we have at
home. But they look like dogs.

Gary: What kind of, can a wolf climb a tree?

JL: (thinking aloud) Can a wolf climb a tree? I don't know. I don't think
so, Gary, but we can look that up when you come to The Book Place,
'cause I have an encyclopedia. Try to remember that one, OK? and

we'll look it up. Here we go. (reading) "Back at the old den, the cubs
are snuggled deep in shaded sleep. Their bright white ear spots wink
like magic eyes. With rough, wet licks from her long tongue,—"
Kenny: Hey. Hey.
JL: —"the tigress stirs them awake."
Kenny: I see something white. White. That's their skin.
Gary: It's a white tiger.
Kenny: White tigers aren't real.
Gary: Yeah, they are.
JL: But they live in a special part of the world, in just one part.
Gary: White tigers are real.
JL: (reading) "Grooming keeps their fur sleek and clean." I'm glad your
mamas don't lick you to make you clean. Think about that.
Gary: White tigers are. White tigers are alive.
JL: They are, and they live in one particular part of the world. But did ya
ever think about different ways of getting clean? What if your mama
licked you to get you clean?
Gary: eeeewwwww (rhymes with "you")
JL: But that's what cats do, and that's what big cats like tigers do too. . . .

JL: Here's the fact part. I didn't read the fact part. (reading) "No one
knows for sure why tigers have ear spots. They may help small cubs to
follow their mother. Or perhaps they are flashed as a warning to other
tigers." So we don't know *why* they have ear spots, but we know they
do have ear spots.
Kenny: I know why they have ear spots.
JL: Why is that?
Kenny: When they wiggle their ears, it makes the cubs go over there. And
it tells the other tigers that someone's gonna attack them.
JL: I see. Kind of a warning system . . .

JL: (reading) "The cubs are 6 months old now. When they are older, their
claws will cut deep into the hardest wood or the tough hide of their
prey." Their claws could just cut right into that table. That table is made
of wood. But not when they're little ones like this [i.e., not until they are
older].
Gary: Can they cut into the wall?
JL: I think so, 'cause the wall is probably softer than the table is. Here's
the facts part. (reading) "Tigers find their own territory, which they
mark by scratching trees and rocks and by leaving their scent—"
Kenny: I know, I know why they said they leave their mark.

JL: Why?

Kenny: Because of they make a triangle and that means go that way. [He seems to be describing markings on a trail for hikers to follow.]

JL: Well, that's another way of marking. That's a way of marking for people. (Reading continues about the mother and two cubs, now grown, killing a wild pig and then going for a swim)

JL: The fact part tells us that tigers are among the few big cats to enjoy swimming. I didn't know that.

Gary: I didn't know that.

Wesley: I'm glad you're reading the facts. . . .

JL: Here we are at the end. You know what's going to happen. (reading) "The tigress has taught the two cubs all her tricks. Now, at eighteen months, they must find their own homes without her. A pattern of gliding stripes slides into the trees—"

Chad: And she disappears.

JL: "—and the mother disappears." You even remembered that word, Chad.

There is nothing robotic about these children's responses to this text. They engage with *Tigress* in a variety of ways, including

- Relating their own prior knowledge to the text (e.g., "snakes could be under there").
- Evaluating their own knowledge in relation to this text (e.g., "I didn't know that").
- Identifying with characters (e.g., "If I was in that tall grass . . .").
- Projecting beyond the text (e.g., "Tigers would like to play hide and seek").
- Making logical connections (e.g., "It would be dangerous because . . .").
- Observing—"reading"—illustrations (e.g., "I see something white." "It's a white tiger").
- Inquiring (e.g., "Can a wolf climb a tree?" "Can they cut into the wall?").

But however diverse their responses, they are real: They carry out the children's own communication purposes. They are authentic responses to an authentic text.

Tigress invites an efferent response. Often, the read-aloud is one that especially invites an aesthetic response, whether fairy tale or takeoff (e.g., *The Three Little Wolves and the Big, Bad Pig* [Trivizas, 1993]; *Prince Cinders* [Cole, 1987]), a realistic story (e.g., *Jamaica Louise James* [Hest, 1996];

Amazing Grace [Hoffman, 1991]), a playful story (e.g., *Something Might Happen* [Lester, 2003]; *Don't Let the Pigeon Drive the Bus* [Willems, 2003]; *Tacky, the Penguin* [Lester, 1988]), a thought-provoking story (e.g., *Fritz and the Beautiful Horses* [Brett, 1981]; *Tico and the Golden Wings* [Lionni, 1964]; *The Quilt Maker's Gift* [Brumbeau, 2000]), a poetic story (e.g., *'Possum Come a-Knockin'* [Van Laan, 1992]), or a folktale (e.g., *Luba and the Wren* [Polacco, 1999]); *It Could Always Be Worse* [Zemach, 1976]). Whatever the specific type, these are instances of literature crafted toward the reader's/listener's engagement during the reading event. And indeed, many of the children's verbal responses suggest an aesthetic orientation.

- Spoiled Princess Penelope (Lester, 1996) regularly hurls insults at her pet parrot. Wesley collapses with laughter over each insult: "Bird Brain!" "Big Beak!" "Knothead!"
- Beatrice (Numeroff, 2004) is giving her older brother grief. He has to take her with him to the public library while he tries to write a report for homework. She hates the library and is being quite unpleasant. Dennis (7 years old, kindergarten) says, "I don't like Beatrice!"
- Jody and I have read *Gossie* (Dunrea, 2002)—the story of a "small yellow gosling" who "likes to wear bright, red boots. Every day."—together several times. Jody hugs the book to her chest and says dreamily, "I just love *Gossie.*"

These children are experiencing real efferent and aesthetic literary orientations. The literature is authentic, and it evokes authentic responses.

Here is a quite different example from a K/1 classroom in another state that I visited regularly for several months a few years ago. Several months into the school year, the reading supervisor started exerting pressure on the classroom teacher because he did not see sufficient evidence that the teacher was teaching the objectives that would one day appear on the high-stakes standardized test. The supervisor required the teacher to start spending X minutes a day doing what he called "word work." Enter a set of phonics-oriented books, including *A Snack for Mack* (Hollander, 2002), which came to be known as the -ack book. In the -ack book, a boy leaves various "-ack" objects in various "-ack" locations (his backpack by the track, etc.) and his dog named Mack brings each object back, except for the boy's snack, which Mack eats. The teacher didn't like this book (and the others in the series), but she felt pressured to read it to the children. I listened to the reading and was not surprised that the children greeted it with silence. There were none of the laughter, observations, connections, and wonderings that I had heard them express when the teacher had read them *Millions of Cats* (Ga'g, 1928/1996) or *The Five Chinese Brothers* (Bishop & Wiese, 1938). The -ack book is a pedagogical contrivance, not literature. It is phonics drill masquerading as story, and the children seemed to know the difference.

THE SOCIAL THRUST OF EARLY WRITING

Listen to Cyndy Hoffman, a K/1 teacher, as she talks about her students' early writing:

> I want [my students] to write; I don't want them to spell words. I want them to use words. Writing needs to be a friend, and it needs to be a tool. And that's what my job is: to help them know this. (Lindfors & Townsend, 1999, p. 17)

Cyndy is talking about authenticity here: Writing is a tool to carry out the child's communication work.

You remember from the last chapter that the child in a one-word stage uses single word utterances as social tools. Those single words are not just verbal noises; they are moves in social interaction, such as asserting ("mine"), requesting ("more"), connecting ("hi," "bye-bye"), inquiring (single word spoken with rising intonation), and so on. These are words that enable children to manage their relations with others.

A similar social, connecting thrust is also evident in children's early writing.

> Kelly (2 and a half) scribbles on a sheet of paper, hands it to me, and says, "This is to Morfar" (i.e., it is a note for her grandfather, who is not present). She scribbles on another sheet, hands it to me, and says, "This is to my birthday" (i.e., it is an invitation to her birthday party, still some 6 months away). Scribbles they may be, but they are deliberate communication acts that carry out her social purposes.

> While her mother is out, a 6-year-old gets into her mother's sewing basket. She leaves this note:
> "Dar Mom
>   Im sre for gedin inde uor sduf. Doby mad." (Dear Mom, I'm sorry for getting into your stuff. Don't be mad.) (Newkirk, 1984, p. 343)

In many K/1 classrooms, teachers affix printed labels to objects in the room: table, chair, window, and so on. But Carol Avery tells us that when she did this, it did not have the effect she intended.

I remember Lisa, a first grader from years ago who one day in late March pointed to a word taped to the window and asked, "Mrs. Avery, why's that word on the window?" The word: *window*. I'd taped it there in August and Lisa had no idea what it said or *why* it was there. (Avery, 2002, pp. 55–56).

Yet in the K/1 classrooms I know, children are extremely attentive to another kind of label that they find in their classroom: classmates' names on cubbies. We often hear the children make spontaneous observations like these:

- Pointing to the letter "J" in an alphabet display, the child says, "That one is Jenny's." (i.e., Jenny's name begins with that letter.)
- Copying the title of the book he is taking from The Book Place, *Dinosaurs*, Jeremy points to the first letter and says, "Danny has that."

Why are the labels "Jenny" and "Danny" so salient to the child? Why do these labels capture the child's attention in a way that "table" and "window" do not? After all, the labels all look the same: black letter sequences on white rectangular cards. It's the social possibilities that make the difference. A "table" is just a wooden object, but "Jenny" and "Danny" are potential friends. Words are social tools: spoken words, written words.

Given young children's social orientation, perhaps it is no surprise that letter-/note-writing is often an early writing engagement for children. Letter-writing is very close to talk. It is dialogic and conversational, and talk, as we know, is what young children do best. Writing notes to friends is perhaps but a small next step into written expression.

Zoe (5 years old, kindergarten) wrote a note to her teacher and carefully placed it on the teacher's chair, where she was sure the teacher would find it when she came in that morning: "ms. marion your THE BEST TEACHEr EVER LOVE, Zoe"

Various games and writing materials are available in the cafeteria at breakfast time so the children have something to do if they finish breakfast before it is time to go to the classroom. Sometimes children choose to write to me (as I write to them each day). Molly (7 years old, 2nd grade) writes, "I like the Book Plae. and makivng books Love. Molly (She draws five hearts around the edge.)

Jody writes me a letter, too. (See Figure 2.1.)

Jonah sent an e-mail message to me when I was absent (carless) for several days. (See Figure 2.2.)

Figure 2.1. Jody's note

Figure 2.2. Jonah's e-mail

Dear Ms. Judy,

when will   you   cume back   to   school   I   miss   you

Ms. Judy   because   I   wot   to   reod   weth   you   ples
cumbac

tomorrow

from

Each of these notes is carrying out the child's intention to connect. In this, young children are doing what they have been doing, literally, from birth: connecting with others through their (verbal and/or preverbal) expression.

COPYING: COMMUNICATION OR EXERCISE?

Deciding which instances of writing are authentic (communicatively purposeful for the child) and which are not can be tricky because sometimes the two look very similar on the surface, though they are deeply different.

Remember how *Blue Hat, Green Hat* (Boynton, 1995) and *Knock Knock* (Gref, 2002), like the labels "table" and "Jenny," seemed so much alike on the surface, but at that deep level of authenticity—purpose—they were quite different. The same can be true of early writing. Consider this example:

> Deshawna (5 years old, kindergarten) tells me she wants to write a letter to her mother. She takes a sheet of note paper, writes her own name on it, and then copies from the cover of a book: "The Little Mermaid." She folds the paper and puts it in an envelope to take home to her mother.

Deshawna copied the book title, no doubt about it. But she didn't do this as an exercise; she did this as a communication move: a letter to her mom. This is what toddlers do when their language consists of single-word sentences. They say the same words they have heard others say, but they are not just imitating; they use these words to enter and maintain conversations (e.g., to call an adult's attention to something and, thus, start a conversation). This is a good example of a language-acquisition strategy that one researcher has called "Make the most of what you've got." (Fillmore, 1976). It's a good description of what Deshawna is doing. She copies instances of print around her and makes them into a letter to mom. And her mom will respond to it as a letter; she will respond to her daughter's communicative intention.

Consider the following contrasting pair of examples, both of which involve copying (i.e., the child replicating a model as closely as possible). One is authentic and one is not.

Example 1

> I am observing a 1st-grade classroom in which the teacher is reading *Charlotte's Web* (White, 1952) to the children, one chapter each morning. After reading each chapter, the teacher gives every child a sheet with an outline of a pig with horizontal lines inside for the child to write on. On the board, she has written a short summary of the chapter for that day (two or three sentences), and the children copy the summary onto the pig sheet.

Example 2

> At the entrance to The Book Place there is a sign-out book, a spiral notebook that sits on top of a low bookshelf between a tin of pencils and a large straw basket in which the children place the books they are returning.

When the child and I enter The Book Place to read together, the child returns her book to the basket, then checks off her last entry in the sign-out
book (the entry for the book she has just returned). We read and/or write
together for a while, and then the child selects a new book to take back to
her classroom. She writes her name in the sign-out book, and beside her
name she writes—most often, copies—the title of the book she is taking.

These are two instances of copying, so similar but so different. As you
can see, the difference is authenticity—the significance of each instance
for the child—or what she sees herself as doing.

It would be a mistake to say that copying in the sign-out book has a
purpose and copying in the *Charlotte's Web* sheet does not. I'm sure that,
for the teacher, the *Charlotte's Web* sheet did have a purpose, though I'm
not sure what it was. Did she intend this as a handwriting exercise? Or
as a support for comprehension of the chapter she had just read? I don't
know what her purpose was, but I do know that it was *her* purpose, not
the children's. And that, of course, is the crucial issue: Children learn from
where *they* are, not from where *we* are. The communication purposes that
are relevant to their learning are their purposes, not ours. The children
know that the writing they do in the sign-out book is real; it will be used.
They write their entries so that we will remember what books they have
taken from The Book Place. They know this because it's what we do.
Time and again I come to the classroom to take a child with me to The
Book Place, and I ask, "Do you have a book to bring back?" Silence. She's
thinking. Can't remember. "Well, that's OK," I tell her. "We'll look in the
sign-out book." And that is what we do. In contrast, the *Charlotte's Web*
sheet will be checked off ("She did it OK" or "She didn't do it OK") and
thrown away—not read, not used.

Initially, the sign-out book was for me. As the child and I left The
Book Place to return the child to her classroom, I would hastily jot down
the child's name and the title of the book she was taking. Soon I saw that
the children could take this job on themselves. Of course! (Why didn't I
see it sooner?) Slight rearrangements made this child-friendly: placing the
sign-out book and a container of pencils on a low shelf within the child's
reach, providing enough space for the child to lay down the book whose
title she was copying, and so forth. My purpose in making these changes
was pedagogical: I wanted to engage the children in a purposeful writing experience. However, the recording/recalling purpose of the sign-out
book quickly became the children's: They refer to the sign-out book when
they can't remember what book they have taken.

The sign-out book is not beautiful to look at. Figure 2.3 shows an example (with the children's names deleted). But beautiful or not, it works (literally!) for us. Here, again, written language is a tool.

Figure 2.3. Sample page from the sign-out book

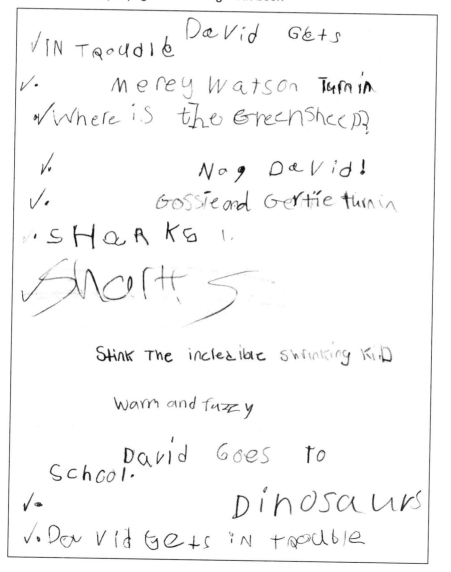

THE AUTHENTICITY OF WRITING WORKSHOP

With his seminal book, *Writing: Teachers and Children at Work* (1983), Donald Graves introduced the writing workshop, an approach to the teaching of writing that has become a staple in many classrooms. Since 1983, much has been written about using this approach with students of all ages, but some educators/authors (most notably Carol Avery, 2002) have focused explicitly on using this approach with young children—emergent and early developmental readers and writers. Authenticity is the heart and soul of writing workshop: Children write to carry out their communication purposes; they write to be published; they write to be read. You are probably already familiar with this approach to the teaching of writing, but consider the authenticity of the *process* involved.

- The child writes every day (if possible) during a regularly scheduled, substantial writing period (45–60 minutes).
- The child writer moves through topic selection, drafting, revising, editing, and publishing of selected pieces of writing.
- The workshop each day typically includes a minilesson, a block of time for writing (and conferencing with others about the writing), and a sharing time.

You can see that the child is a real writer, doing what real authors do, including interacting with fellow writers in a writing community.

Now consider the authenticity of the *principles* that guide this process.

- *Ownership:* The child writes for her purposes, on her selected topics, in her own voice.
- *Community:* The child is supported by members of the writing community (teacher and children) in ongoing conferencing, sharing, and celebration.
- *Guidance:* Through ongoing conferences, minilessons, and evaluation, the teacher consciously, sensitively, and responsively helps children write more effectively and more diversely over time.

Clearly, there are pedagogical purposes here, but the ongoing writing workshop experience—in both its processes and its principles—is designed to be attentive to and supportive of children's own writing purposes, whether to make their readers laugh, scare their readers, tell a story, relive a significant personal experience, explain how something works, inform readers, and so on. Writing workshop is designed to be authentic.

CONNECTING READING AND WRITING, TEXT AND TALK

Routine writing tasks like the sign-out book, continuous engagement in writing workshop, interaction with real literature—all these authentic daily engagements with written language support children as they make written expression their own. These experiences make the child's journey continuous, from oral into written expression of meaning and purpose. There is continuity.

There is also *connection*—connection of oral and written expression. The sign-out book, writing workshop, and and read-aloud all live within a classroom.

- Conversation swirls around the sign-out book. ("Here's my name." "I'll put a check mark here." "I took *Knuffle Bunny*." "I think my book is in my cubby. Or maybe in my backpack.")
- Talk infuses writing workshop—in teacher–child conferences, minilessons, child–child conferences, sharing time.
- It's talk that introduces the book to be read aloud, and it's talk that sustains and extends it. It lives in the shared comments and observations and wonderings—all talk.

Oral and written language come together in a natural way, just as they did in Marion Coffee's kindergarten problem-solving discussion.

You may have noticed another connection, too: the connection between reading and writing. The sign-out book, letters to friends, and writing workshop are as much about reading as they are about writing: When you create written text, you read it as you go, and perhaps again as you reflect on the finished product. Some educators have gone so far as to suggest that children learn to read by writing and that they learn to write by reading.

WRITING TO CONNECT WITH OTHERS: THE CASE OF MARIA

Maria was with us for almost 3 months, twice as long as most of our students. She was 6 years old when she arrived: a strong, affectionate, resilient 1st grader who was a forceful presence in the classroom—and a loud one! Whenever she was unhappy and couldn't have her own way (as was often the case in those early days), she would wail. The teacher and children would go about their business as usual. Often, Maria's unhappiness had to do with friendship. She wailed when Annette said she wouldn't be her friend and she wailed when she couldn't have the same (meatless) kind of spaghetti that Helen's mother (a vegetarian) had brought to the lunchroom for her daughter's lunch.

Maria very soon discovered that she could learn to read and write, and there was nothing she wanted more. All her strength and determination got channeled right into her attempts to crack the written code as we read together on The Book Place couch. Book after book, we read together—books that invited her engagement and participation. And participate she did: listening to my reading first, soon chiming in, then taking on part, then all, of the reading/telling herself. Soon she was pointing at the words as she read. Miscues were high-quality: When we read *Gossie*, she read "gosling" for "Gossie," "frontwards" for "foreward," "up the hill" for "uphill"; when we read *Rosie's Walk* (Hutchins, 1971), she read "through the fence" for "through the gate" and "past the milk" for "past the mill" (she apparently saw the white flour pouring from the mill in the picture as milk); and when we read *Cookie's Week* (Ward, 1988), instead of reading "Cookie upset the trash can" she read "Cookie bothered the trash can." She knew she was successful. "I'm so smart," she told me. This from the child who had spent most of her early days under the table wailing! When word reached me that Maria's mother had asked, "Who is this 'Miss Judy' who writes the notes Maria brings home?" I knew that Maria's mother was reading my daily notes with her daughter.

It was letter-writing that became Maria's way into writing. Of course! She was a deeply affectionate and connecting child. Her first note was to me: "How do you write 'Dear Miss Judy?'" she asked. A second note, written on her own, followed a few days later. I asked her if she'd like to write a book about herself. "Yes," she said. So we read some books in preparation (*I Like Me!* [Carlson, 1990], *I'm Gonna Like Me!* [Curtis, 2002], *Today I Feel Silly* [Curtis, 1998]), and soon she wrote her first book: *About Me*. She cried a few weeks later when she thought she had lost it and was hugely relieved when she found it. One day soon after, I found her crying at breakfast. "I want my mom," she told me. "I miss my mom. I love my mom." I told her that when she came to The Book Place with me that morning, I'd have note paper ready in case she wanted to write a letter to her mom. She did. "Dear Mom I love you," she wrote at the top. Then, "Love Maria [surname]" at the bottom. After some thought and conversation, in the middle of the page she wrote that she had been crying but was happy now.

After Maria left our class to enter public school, she wrote me eight letters. Here are the first and fourth:

Dear Mrs. Judy,
I LOVE you very much.
Have a Happy Holiday. and
God Bless you.
I will miss you alot, when I
go to my new school. Please
write to me My address
is: [address]
Love your ~~Frnd~~
   1 Friend
Maria
PS Thank you For
Everything

Dear Miss Judy
I love the Velentine
gift you gove me! Thank
you so much I love my libra
ry card. I hope to see you again
soon. I love you very much.
I miss you very much
Write back to me agai-
n
Love you—Miss Judy
Maria

Maria found her own way into written language: her way, her purposes, in tune with her personality. Nothing was more important to Maria than maintaining and fostering friendship. Writing served this end for her.

When I think of Maria, Cyndy's words echo: "Writing needs to be a friend, and it needs to be a tool."

For Maria, writing was both. It was authentic.

CHAPTER 3

Meaning-Orientation

This chapter begins with Deshawna and Annette, who demonstrate a sharp contrast between a meaning-orientation and a code-orientation toward print. We go on to consider the child's meaning-orientation in her oral language and to question some notions about oral and written language that underlie much of the literacy instruction we see today. Shamiya brings us back into the classroom, and there we focus on literature. We end, once again, with connections.

MEANING-ORIENTATION VERSUS CODE-ORIENTATION TO PRINT: DESHAWNA AND ANNETTE

Deshawna (5 years old) and I are sitting on the couch in The Book Place, reading *No, David!* together (Shannon, 1998). The book is new to her. We get to the page where David is streaking down the street with no clothes on. She squeals, "He butt neked! He showin' his booty!"

Annette (7 years old, 2nd grade) and I are sitting on the couch in The Book Place reading *Ginger* (Voake, 1997), the story of a cat. Annette has chosen this book because she loves stories about cats. The book is too hard for her to read herself. I read it to her and then she chooses several pages to read to me. She has trouble with some of the words, especially the function words (e.g., "helping verbs") and, as usual, she goes immediately to her preferred (only?) strategy: sounding out. One page shows Ginger in a basket, and the text says that the girl Ginger belongs to gave Ginger a beautiful basket "where he would curl up."
Annette: wuh er . . . wuh er (She looks at me for help)
JL: Where
Annette: where he . . . wuh ul duh . . . wuh ul duh (She looks at me blankly)
JL: (rhythmically) "Where he hmmmm curl up." Can you think what that would be? "Where he hmmmmm curl up."
Annette: (Silence)

Later in the story, Ginger is gone and the little girl says, "I hope he hasn't run away."

> *Annette:* I ho, hope he . . . ha ss n t; ha ss n t. (She looks at me blankly. Removed from a meaning focus, the sound sequences unlock nothing for her.)

Deshawna and Annette are different in a number of ways. They have had different life experiences, including the experience of domestic violence that has brought them to SafePlace. Annette, just starting 2nd grade, has had 2 years of formal schooling; Deshawna, a beginning kindergartner, has had none.

One important difference between them is the way they approach the page. They come with quite different expectations for what they will find there and how they are to engage with it. Deshawna comes to the page orienting to what it's about, what's happening. Her focus is on meaning. Annette comes asking what the sounds/words are to be spoken correctly one by one, left to right, line by line. It is as if Annette is watching slides and Deshawna is watching a film. For Annette, each word—even each letter sound—seems to be a separate and discrete event: word, word, word. She does not bring to bear her language knowledge, which should help her figure out function words. Function words belong in flowing sequences, but there are few flowing sequences for Annette, just unconnected words. When I try to get her to tune in to the flow of the language she knows so well, she doesn't do it. It is as if reading is something other than language. For Deshawna, however, there is flow; something is happening, there is action in progress.

Written language, like oral language, includes both the meanings we express and the code we use to express them. But for Annette, in written language, the code has become the whole. For her, the code does not serve meaning; it has replaced it. For Annette, reading doesn't include the code; it *is* the code. Annette is oriented toward making sounds; she is not oriented toward making sense.

MEANING-ORIENTATION IN ORAL LANGUAGE

How different this is from what Annette does when she talks to other people. When she talks, she makes sounds and does so systematically. She selects the appropriate phonemes (basic sounds) and pronounces them correctly (using the right place in the mouth with the tongue in the proper position and the stream of air moving continuously for phonemes like /s/

and /f/, stopping for phonemes like /p/ and /k/, passing through the nose and mouth for phonemes like /m/ and /n/, stopping and then releasing for the initial phonemes in "judge" and "church"). She modifies her pronunciation of each phoneme appropriately in various combinations, shaping each one to the phoneme that precedes or follows it. For example, she pronounces /p/ with a puff of air (aspiration) in "pill" but not in "spill," and she lengthens the vowel sound in "cad," but not in "cat." She varies the "tunes" of her sentences appropriately—the rhythms, stress patterns, intonation (the ups and downs of the voice that sometimes differentiate questions and statements). And, of course, she combines phonemes into words and word combinations that convey what she wishes to say. She does all this quite unconsciously, just as adults do when we talk to one another. Like Annette, we tend to focus on meaning—on *what* we are saying, not *how*.

It might seem that we are unaware of the code we use when we talk to one another because it has become automatic. It is so familiar that it has become transparent, whereas the written code, on the other hand, would be the focus of attention for a child who is just learning to read and write. This is surely a reasonable supposition. But when we look at oral language development, we see that, from the beginning, when the system is completely new to the child, she orients toward meaning (connection, communication), not form, and she learns the code (form) along the way.

From early infancy, the baby expresses through smiles, gestures, and body language. The beginnings of speech—oral expression—are in evidence, too. Babies make vocal sounds from the beginning, but after a few months, they produce strings of repeated consonant–vowel sound combinations (babababa, mamamama). When, toward the end of the child's 1st year, the mother enters the baby's room to get him up from his nap and the baby gives a big smile, reaches his arms up toward his mother, and says, "Mama," his mother knows that "Mama" is a word, not babble. "Mama" has meaning for child and mother both. (This sequence from random vocalizations, to patterned babbling, to words may remind you of the child's later writing sequence from scribbles, to letter forms, to invented spelling.) And you will remember from Chapter 1 that the infant's single words—spoken within a present, shared context—have the import of sentences.

"'gain"—I want to do this again.
"no"—I don't want to eat that.
"doggie" (spoken with rising intonation)—Is that a doggie?
"down"—It fell down from my high chair.

From the beginning, whether by gesture, word, or word combinations, young children use whatever means they have to communicate. They are meaning-oriented: They have messages to convey and they do that, and they attend and respond to the messages of others. They seem quite unaware of the forms they are using. Even when adults try to draw the young child's attention to form, his focus on meaning seems to persist:

> *Child:* Nobody don't like me.
> *Mother:* No, say "nobody likes me."
> *Child:* Nobody don't like me.
> *(eight repetitions of this dialogue)*
> *Mother:* No, now listen carefully, say "*nobody likes me.*"
> *Child:* Oh! Nobody don't like*S* me.
>   (Lindfors, 1987, p. 102; quoting McNeill, 1966, p. 69)

> *Child:* Want other one spoon, Daddy.
> *Father:* You mean, you want THE OTHER SPOON.
> *Child:* Yes, I want other one spoon, please, Daddy.
> *Father:* Can you say "the other spoon"?
> *Child:* Other . . . one . . . spoon.
> *Father:* Say "other."
> *Child:* Other.
> *Father:* Spoon.
> *Child:* Spoon.
> *Father:* Other . . . spoon.
> *Child:* Other . . . spoon. Now give me other one spoon?
>   (Lindfors, 1987, p. 102; quoting Braine, 1971, pp. 160–61)

Yet, remarkably, over time, while focusing on meaning, the child learns form—the mechanisms for expressing herself the way adults in her community do.

FOUR QUESTIONABLE NOTIONS
ABOUT ORAL AND WRITTEN LANGUAGE

What has brought Annette to this point where a focus on sound sequences (forms) has replaced a focus on meaning? Her form focus is in direct conflict with her experience of oral language. Why does she apparently see spoken language as communication, but written language as letters/sounds marching across the page? Part of the answer may be that there is a tendency for many adults in Annette's world (and in ours) to see the two—oral and written language—quite differently. It is inevitable that our notions of oral and written language will find their way into our classrooms, informing the decisions we make about how we teach children to read and write.

Many adults feel that when a child learns to talk she is learning to communicate, whereas when she is learning to read and write she is learning to decode. Of course, both oral language and written language include code: the expressive system (the verbal sounds of speech, the letter forms of print). The question is, What is the role of code learning? Many adults see the place of code learning differently in oral and in written language learning: Is it the whole task, or is it a part of something larger, a means to the end of communication? My guess is that Annette's 1st-grade teacher believed that Annette's (main? sole?) task in becoming a reader/writer was to learn to decode. Annette's teacher may also have held other notions about the differences between oral and written language—questionable but quite pervasive notions about regularity, complexity, naturalness, and alphabetic principle. In the four sections below, I state these notions and challenge the conventional "wisdom" of each one.

Notion 1—Regularity: Unlike oral English, written English is problematic in its irregularity—its lack of perfect, one-to-one sound/letter correspondence.

We are acutely aware of instances of irregularity in the written system, and we assume that these pose challenges for the child learning to read and write. We point to one sound being represented by different letters (*s*ugar, *Ch*icago, *sh*oe; r*ai*n, r*ei*n, s*a*ne; t*o*, t*wo*, t*oo*), one spelling representing different sounds (th*ough*t, thr*ough*; w*i*nd, w*i*nd; d*oe*s, d*oe*s; *th*in, *th*is; r*ea*d, r*ea*d), some letters representing no sound at all (*k*nee, *k*now), and so on. How convenient it would be, we think, if "s" always and only "said" /s/, if /š/ were always and only spelled "sh." We may long for perfect letter/sound matching, assuming that the child would quickly learn to pronounce the right sound sequences and meaning would instantly and automatically follow. The child would not have to deploy his mind toward meaning: Meaning would just be there if his verbal noises were right.

Yes, the lack of perfect one-to-one sound/letter match looms large for many adults interested in children's literacy development. What we often fail to realize is that spoken English is, if anything, more "mismatched" (irregular) than written English. Yet the child learning English as her mother tongue does not seem troubled by the lack of perfect pattern.

- There is a pattern of reversing the subject of a sentence and the first verbal element when we change statements to questions:
  –He can go → Can he go?
  –He is going → Is he going?
  –He can go tomorrow → When can he go?
  –He is going to school → Where is he going?
  But this pattern doesn't work with simple verbs.
  –*He came*, but not *Came he* or *When came he?*
  These verbs require *do* forms (do, does, did). These forms don't "mean" anything really; they just have to be there.
- The pattern for forming the past tense is to add /əd/ to verbs ending with /t/ or /d/ (melt → melt + /əd/, plod → plod + /əd/); to add /t/ to verbs ending with voiceless sounds (walk → walk + /t/, fuss → fuss + /t/); and to add /d/ to verbs ending with voiced sounds (wave → wave + /d/, wag → wag + /d/). But the past tense of "see" is "saw" (not "seed"); the past tense of "think" is "thought" (not "thinked"); the past tense of "put" is "put" (not "putted"); the past tense of "come" is "came" (not "comed").
- The pattern for forming plurals is to add /əz/ to nouns ending in /s/ or /z/ (bus → bus + /əz/); to add /s/ to nouns ending with unvoiced sounds (cake → cake + /s/, hat → hat + /s/); and to add /z/ to nouns ending with voiced sounds (spoon → spoon + /z/, sofa → sofa + /z/). The plural of "house" is "houses," but the plural of "mouse" is not "mouses"; the plural of (tin) "can" is "cans," but the plural of "man" is not "mans." The plural of "deer" is "deer," not "deers."
- Comparative forms usually add -er to adjectives: "lovelier," "prettier," "bigger," "smaller"—but not "gooder" or "badder."
- The ending -er (sometimes spelled -or) can also indicate a doer: A baker is someone who bakes; an actor is someone who acts; a teacher is someone who teaches; a singer is someone who sings; a supervisor is someone who supervises. But someone who cooks is a chef, not a cooker, and a doctor is not someone who "docts." We can replay or regain something, but we can't "refix" something, nor can we "rejump." We can undo something, but we can't "unmend" or "unsew" something.
- We can say "I saw him go," but not "I want him go." We have to put "to" in the second sentence in order for the sentence to be grammatical (rather like the written "k" in "know"; it doesn't "sound," but it just has to be there for the word to be written/ spelled conventionally).

- One word can have more than one meaning: a bank is the side of a river or a place to keep your money; a fire is a blaze, and to fire someone is to take his job away; a book is something to read, and to book someone is to bring a charge against him. And one meaning can be expressed by more than one word (*small, little, tiny*).
- Whole sentences can have more than one meaning:
  –Did you ever see a house fly?
  –They are eating apples.
  –Visiting relatives can be a nuisance.

We could go on and on with examples, but the question is, Do these examples mean that oral expression is chaotic? Not at all. It is patterned, and as we saw in Chapter 1, the child learning to talk picks up on the patterns and uses them to communicate. Her early two- and three-word sentences reflect the word order patterns of adult speech; her overregularized forms (*comed, mans, putted, mouses*) are applications of plural and past-tense patterns. But like written expression, oral expression, though patterned, is not rigidly so. Both systems (oral and written) are patterned with variation. If we are more aware of (and troubled by) the variation in written language, it may be because we *use* oral language, but tend to *analyze* written language.

Deshawna and Annette have both learned the pattern-with-variation system of oral language. Now they are learning the pattern-with-variation system of written language. Why would we expect the variation in the second to be problematic, when the greater variation in the first was not? And why would we assume that Deshawna and Annette would come to written language expecting it to be a different kind of system (rigidly patterned) than oral expression? After all, both are language.

The variation in the code of written expression may be more problematic for adults, who analyze the system, than it is for children, who acquire it.

Notion 2–Complexity: Learning to read and write is more complex (and difficult) than learning to speak (or use sign language) and listen.

Some might argue that learning to speak a language must be easier than learning to read and write it because (1) a child does this first, and does it without formal tutoring; and (2) everyone learns to speak a language, but not everyone learns to read and write one. Indeed, some languages have no written system at all or have developed one only recently (e.g., Navajo, some African languages). However, these facts are better explained by social reasons than cognitive ones. Early encounters—whether for a society or for a child—are face-to-face. And so we talk to one another, and in that everyday world infused with talk, the child creates a system of oral expression like the one he hears others in his community using. It is not a matter of which expressive system is easier or more difficult to learn, but rather, which one serves our communication purposes. And our earliest purposes are served by talk.

Recall from the last chapter that the child has an innate capacity for language: Children are born with the general structures of human language "given," and they must figure out the specifics, that is, the particular language of the community into which they are born. This innate capacity is a *language* capacity. It would be counterintuitive to suggest that the child's innate language structure is relevant to the acquisition of oral expression but not written expression, and therefore, learning to speak (or sign) is easier than learning to read and write. Oral and written language are both *language*, and that is what the child is geared for.

Consider what the K/1 child has already accomplished when he begins formal literacy instruction in school. He has already learned

- How his community categorizes objects, actions, feelings, and characteristics
- The labels (words) for these categories
- Words and parts of words that carry out grammatical functions (e.g., -ly, -ness, -ed, -s, to, do)
- How to put the words and word parts together to express syntactic relationships (use of word order and affixes)
- How to produce the sounds (or signs) and sound combinations that express meanings
- How to use words to carry out different communication purposes
- How to adapt speech to be appropriate in different social situations

Now he comes to formal literacy instruction and all this is the same. He already knows the words, meanings, structures, relationships, social purposes, and so forth—the *language* that he will find on the printed page. All he has to do now is learn a second expressive system for the linguistic, cognitive, social knowledge he already has. Learning that "c-a-t" represents the particular animal you call a /kæt/ seems less formidable than having to learn what a /kæt/ is (what is included in that category and what is excluded), how to say /kæt/, how /kæt/ combines with other words when you want to say something about a cat, how to talk about cats in different social situations and for different purposes, and so on.

Obviously, becoming a real reader and writer entails far more than figuring out how the basic system of print works. Readers and writers engage with and create many kinds of texts in many styles and serving many purposes. But more often than not, those who express the notion that learning to read and write is harder than learning to talk are focusing on the mechanics of literacy, and these, on the face of it, seem fairly simple.

Notion 3–Naturalness: Learning oral language is a spontaneous, natural process; learning written language is a deliberate, structured process.

The dichotomy in this statement (oral language is X, written language is Y) is misleading, for it obscures the fact that both oral and written language learning can be "spontaneous" in some ways and "structured" in others. In both classroom environments and outside environments, there is evidence of structures that take the child language learner into account—that shape to the child. It's especially easy to see this shaping in classrooms. Teachers of young children create environments that they believe will help children become readers and writers. They select objects, activities, and procedures for literacy development. Some 1st-grade classrooms may incline more toward invitations, others more toward assignments; and what some observers might see as teacher interventions, others might see as teacher interference. But whatever the differences from one classroom to the next, we know that each one didn't just happen to be the way it is by accident. It is the way it is by design; it is the result of a shaping hand.

When a child is learning oral language we see some shaping, too. The structure may be less formal than the shaping structure of the classroom, but there is shaping nonetheless. "Motherese" (as it is sometimes called) offers a particularly good example of a pattern of shaping toward the language learning child.

When you listen to adults interacting with infants or toddlers, you may have the sense that they are speaking differently from the way they would if they were conversing with another adult. You would be right. Adult–infant/toddler interaction has been studied extensively, and a number of characteristic features of adult speech have been identified. (These features come from research done primarily with mainstream, middle-class adult–child pairs.) "Motherese" tends to include a higher proportion of shorter sentences and simpler sentences than is typical of adult–adult speech. The sentences the adult addresses to the child are usually well formed, lacking the false starts, repetitions, self-corrections, hemmings-and-hawings typical of conversation between adults. Adults talking to toddlers tend to repeat a lot and do a lot of paraphrasing. The speech often relies heavily on the immediate, present, shared context in which the conversation is taking place. Adults make greater use of body language and greater use of stress and exaggerated intonation contours (i.e., the rise and fall of the voice includes a wider range than we typically use in adult–adult speech). Adults talking to young children often refer to themselves and the child by name, rather than using pronouns (e.g., "Mommy doesn't like that" or "Does Jenny want to go outside?") We also use some special word forms (e.g., "bye-byes," "jammies," "tummy") and ask a great many questions.

When we modify our speech in these (and other) ways in conversations with young children, our goal is not pedagogical. We are not trying to teach the child. We are trying to have a conversation with the child, and we modify our speech so as to make ourselves understood and to help the child participate. Thus, "Motherese" is a structure that supports conversation between an expert and a novice. So although the teacher–student structures of the classroom may be more formal than those of adult–child interaction, and more consciously oriented toward pedagogy, both still bring expert and novice together in ways that support the efforts of the language learning child.

What about the spontaneity—the "naturalness"—in the child's language learning? We know this to be a characteristic of the child's acquisition of oral language. Do we see this in children's literacy acquisition as well? Yes. It's in evidence before the child begins formal literacy instruction in school and also in his print experience outside of the K/1 classroom. How else could it be, given that the child lives in a print-filled world outside of the classroom? It's a world of birthday cards and recipe cards; of menus and bumper stickers; of clothing labels and lines of print running across the bottom of the TV screen; of newspapers, Coke cans, and ice cream cartons; of flyers and junk mail that come to the house; of shopping malls with ads, store names, and labeled store sections; and of religious print—hymns and scripture. And in this print-filled world, we find spontaneous informal reading examples like these:

Three-year-old Matthew and his adult friend are in a department store. Matthew sees a sign hanging above the greeting card counter and explains, "That sign says 'card.'" Seeing the word "luggage" in the luggage department, Matthew tells the adult that the word must be "cases." (Smith, 1985, p. 118)

Four-year-old Sarah and her mother are reading *Sarah's Unicorn* (Coville, 1979).
> *Mother:* (reading) "He will take her on his back, and they will ride to dawn, dancing on the moon beams. Unicorns can do that you know."
> *Sarah:* Is that the word or are you saying it?
> *Mother:* What, honey? "Unicorns can do that?" It's the words in the book.
> *Sarah:* How come?
> *Mother:* Well, that's what the author wanted to write: "Unicorns can do that you know."
> *Sarah:* Unicorns can do that you know.
> *Mother:* Uh-huh. (Lindfors, 1987, p. 78)

Now Sarah and her mother are reading *Just the Thing for Geraldine* (Conford, 1974).
> *Mother:* (reading the title) Just the thing for Geraldine.
> *Sarah:* Just the thing for Geraldine. (pointing to the title word by word) Just . . . the . . . thing . . . for . . . Geraldine. (Lindfors, 1987, pp. 226–227)

Four-year-old Jill and her mother are reading *Curious George Goes to the Hospital* (Rey & Rey, 2001). The picture in the book shows children in hospital beds. Each bed has a name card with the child's name facing the child. Some cards are pictured on the name side, and some are pictured from the back side.
> *Jill:* (pointing to the children whose cards are pictured from the back) Why they don't got their names?
> *Mother:* Well, their names are on those cards but they're going that way. It's on the other side and we can't see in the book. (Lindfors, 1987, p. 78)

And we find writing examples like these:

Four-year-old Kelly wanted to start "nastics" (gymnastics) at her daycare. She came home disappointed. She had not gotten to start that day because her mother had forgotten to sign the required form for Kelly to give to her teacher. Kelly got paper and pencil, "wrote" (in scribble) a reminder, and handed it to her mother, saying, "Now you can remember to sign the paper so I can go to nastics."

A 5-year-old who is writing a note asks her mother, "Mom, do you spell love l-u-v?" (Schickedanz & Sullivan, 1984, p. 11)

A 5-year-old protects his workbench against intruders by putting a sign above it that reads: DO NAT DSTRB GNYS AT WRK (Bissex, 1980, p. 23)

Are these oral language events? Yes. Are they written language events? Yes. Are they "spontaneous"? Yes. Are they "structured" toward the child learner? Yes. Often, in the child's everyday experience of oral and written language, the simple oral/spontaneous versus written/structured dichotomy doesn't hold up very well.

Notion 4—Alphabetic Principle: Because written English is based on an alphabetic principle, learning to read and write English is a matter of learning the sounds that letters make.

If learning letter sounds were all that reading entailed, how could we account for children like Annette? She looks at print and produces the sound of each letter, but doing this unlocks no story, no image, no information for her. She gets sound, but no sense. Surely, knowledge of letter sounds is a part of what readers and writers know. But if it becomes the whole, we may end up with word callers, not readers.

EARLY SCHOOL LITERACY EXPERIENCE

If this meaning-orientation is such an essential part of the child's language experience from birth, how do we explain Annette's orientation toward print?

I do not know the specifics of Annette's formal literacy instruction during kindergarten and 1st grade, but her approach to print at the beginning of 2nd grade (when she came to SafePlace) suggests that somewhere along the line, she has been reoriented. I must suppose that Annette, like virtually every child who learns her mother tongue, understands language to be about meaning. I must suppose, too, that someone has convinced her that written language is different: Oral language is about meaning, but written language is about form, especially the sounds that letters make. The reorientation has been successful. I worry about Annette.

I do not worry about Shamiya (7-years old). She comes to SafePlace in the last 6 weeks of her 1st-grade year. Shamiya and I go to The Book Place so I can show her around. We walk past the book sets—the shelf of Dr. Seuss books, the Arthur books, the Clifford books, the Curious George books, and so on. Yes, she know these, she tells me. We move on. She spots an Eric Carle book on a nearby shelf and her face lights up. She is delighted. Her teacher has just finished an Eric Carle unit. "Then you must know this book about the hungry caterpillar and this one about the lonely firefly and this one about the busy spider," I say. She does. She tells me that when she left her school to come to SafePlace, her teacher was starting a Kevin Henkes unit. "Then I guess you know *Chrysanthemum* (Henkes, 1991) and *Lilly* (Henkes, 1996). "Oh yes!" she tells me. We take an Eric Carle book from the shelf—one she hasn't read before—and we sit down on the couch to read it together. She takes the book from my hands. Clearly, *she* will do the reading. She does. When she gets stuck on a word, I cover it with my thumb and she reads to the end of the sentence, makes a guess as to what the word might be, and then reads the whole sentence. She makes good guesses—sensible guesses—and, because she is focused on meaning, her knowledge of letter sounds is helpful to her in a way that it isn't for Annette.

Shamiya's literate behavior suggests that her early school literacy experience has been very different from Annette's. It appears that Shamiya's teacher has fostered a meaning-orientation toward print. It's an orientation that is as evident in Shamiya's writing as it is in her reading. Figure 3.1 shows her dialogue journal entry about *Gossie* (Dunrea, 2002), a story about a gosling who loses her beloved red boots, only to find them on the feet of another gosling who becomes her friend. They then share the boots, each gosling wearing one.

You can see that although Shamiya's primary focus has been on meaning, she has also learned much about forms. Of her 42 words in this entry, 32 are spelled conventionally, even though this is an instance of free writing and Shamiya is not focusing on correctness. The 10 words that are not spelled conventionally are close enough that her message is easy to read and understand. It is these 10 words that especially show how Shamiya is relying on her substantial knowledge of letter sounds. The writing suggests that she is also using visual strategies (e.g., the final "e" in "were/ware") and memory (e.g., "away," "took," "friend") as well. So, while Shamiya's main focus in her interactions with print has been on meaning, she has also learned a great deal about forms (e.g., letters, letter sounds), which helps her carry out her purposes and express her meanings in writing. She writes to be read and to be understood, and that means learning how to use the code as more experienced writers do. It means learning form, and Shamiya has.

Figure 3.1. Shamiya's journal entry

I would guess that Shamiya's 1st-grade teacher has not only engaged her students with wonderful literature, but has also provided direct, explicit instruction in the workings of written language: letters, single-letter sounds, letter combinations, punctuation conventions, and so on. Some of this instruction might have come in writing workshop minilessons and conferences, some in small-group guided reading instruction, some in dictation activities, some in whole-class writing events, some in the "shared reading experience" of Big Books (Holdaway, 1979). We can only speculate, but whatever the sources, Shamiya's literate behavior suggests that her teacher held tight to meaning as the goal: It's important to know how the system works because that knowledge unlocks the meaning of texts. For Shamiya's teacher, it was *sense before sound*, both in time and in importance. Let's use Big Books/shared reading experience as an example.

SHARED READING EXPERIENCE

Big Books offer wonderful opportunities for children's engagement in shared reading. If you have ever done shared reading with young children, you know what a remarkable array of observations and comments they make, especially on subsequent readings of a favorite big book such as *The Napping House*. (Wood & Wood, 1984).

- "It's gon' be the mouse next."
- "I can see the tiny flea."
- "I know it's 'napping' 'cuz it starts with N."
- "Yeah, and then it's 'house' 'cuz it starts with Howie's" (i.e., "house" begins with the first letter of Howie's name).
- (Chorus) ". . . in the napping house where everyone is sleeping."

It is all too easy for the teacher to turn shared reading experience into a phonics lesson:

> Here's the book we're going to read today. Here's the title. What do you think this word is? It starts with N. Remember what N says? We talked about that one, remember? /nnnnnnn/ . . . And then that -ing, like in "running" and "walking" and "playing."

I doubt that Shamiya's teacher did this. I am sure she welcomed children's observations about print, even deliberately solicited them, but understood that the book was a story—meaning—first and foremost.

First

Literally first, in time, the teacher introduces the story as a story:

We're going to read this story, *The Napping House*, today. Hmmmm. A napping house? I wonder how a house takes a nap. So who do you think might be sleeping in there? Well, let's see.

She reads all the way through. Probably, by the end of the reading, children are chanting the repeated lines while she sweeps her hand under the print. At some later point, she might comment on the crafting of the text ("What a lot of ways to say somebody's sleeping: 'dozing,' 'slumbering,' . . .") or the print itself (holding the cover toward the children: "I bet some of you figured out that this book is called *The Napping House* even before I told you.") These are invitations for children to share their observations/understandings of the craft and conventions of written language. But the invitation comes after the engagement with this text as story.

Foremost

Attention to form doesn't precede a focus on meaning, nor does it substitute for it or take precedence over it. What *The Napping House* is about is characters piling up on top of each other and trying to sleep, and a grand and glorious collapse. It is not about "n" says /n/. Form serves meaning. Forms are the keys that unlock stories for us; they are not the stories themselves.

Shamiya knows this, Annette does not. Deshawna hasn't started 1st grade yet. When she does, what route will her teacher take?

READ-ALOUD

While teaching at the University of Texas, I often began my Language Arts Methods course by having the students (undergraduates about to begin their student teaching) write down on a 3" × 5" card several of their own elementary school experiences that were special, enduring memories for them. Then they would share these in small groups. Finally, we would discuss them as a whole group. Semester after semester, read-aloud time was the overwhelming treasured memory. One student after another would describe the event as if it were yesterday, recalling the light coming in the classroom window, the special place where the children and teacher sat, the time of day, some of the particular stories read. They remembered warmth; they remembered a sense of community. Later in the semester, when we focused on classroom read-aloud as a topic of study, my students easily generated a list of 20-some reasons to read aloud to children. They spoke of the contribution that read-aloud makes to building community, to demonstrating the teacher's love of reading, to acquainting children with different genres, to expanding children's knowledge of the world, to demonstrating fluent and diverse syntax, to presenting a variety of language styles, to expanding children's vocabulary, and so on.

I wonder why the value that now strikes me as possibly the most important of all for emergent and early developmental readers didn't occur to me or my students then: Every reading of every book reinforces the notion that reading is about meaning. Thus, our read-alouds strengthen the continuity from oral into written language. The meaning orientation that has served the child so well from birth continues to serve him as he moves into written language. Did I miss this because it was so obvious, because it was a "given"?

I may have missed this, but the children I read to do not. Sometimes they make observations about the print on the page—a word they recognize by sight, a word they identify by letter sound, an exclamation mark (they love exclamation marks). But most of their responses are meaning-oriented:

The book is *Tigress* (Dowson, 2004). The tiger, now fully grown, leaves her mother and brother to start her own family. Kenny asks, "Is she afraid?"

The book is *The Three Little Pigs* (Marshall, 1989). I am at the beginning. We have just met the man with a load of straw. Deshawna is anticipating. She is mumbling, "Bricks are comin'. They're comin'. It's gonna be bricks."

Leann and I are reading *Gossie* (Dunrea, 2002) together. She tells me that if Gossie wears her boots every day, "they gonna be a mess."

Alejandro often chooses books about dinosaurs when he comes to The Book Place to read with me. We look at the pictures as I paraphrase the rather dense text for this 5-year-old. We are looking at a picture of two young dinosaurs in some sort of physical engagement (fighting? playing?). Alejandro sees the two as siblings: "He roughhouses with his little brother, but he pretends he's little so he won't hurt him." We look at another picture and I tell him the mother dinosaur in the picture is feeding her baby some berries. (The berries are clustered along a vine.) Alejandro has a different interpretation: "She has a string of beads—a necklace for her little girl dinosaur."

CONNECTING MEANING-ORIENTATION AND AUTHENTICITY

Notice how meaning and purpose go together. The authentic writing engagements from the last chapter—routine writing tasks, letter-writing, writing workshop—are all meaning-oriented as well as authentic (carrying out the child's communication purposes): They convey messages. And the difference between real literature and the -ack book is not only that one is communicatively purposeful and the other is not; it is also that the one is truly about something, and the other is only pretending to be. It makes sense to say, "This book is about Gossie losing her cherished boots" or "This book is about Rosie the hen escaping from the fox." It does not make sense to say, "This book is about -ack." Of course, the author of *A Snack for Mack* (Hollander, 2002) would say that it is about Mack's dog eating his snack, but we know better, and children do, too. That's why they respond so differently to *A Snack for Mack* and *Gossie* (Dunrea, 2002).

Notice, too, that the focal literacy engagements of this chapter—Shared Reading Experience, read-aloud—are authentic as well as meaning-oriented. This connection between meaning and purpose is inevitable: We talk, read, and write about something for some purpose.

And once again, there is the oral language/written language connection. Shared Reading Experience and read-alouds offer the perfect context for bringing oral and written language together: text and talk—that connection that is so supportive of children's literacy acquisition.

LOOKING AHEAD

By now, you might be thinking, Yes, the child's oral language from birth carries out real communication purposes, and this can continue to be the case as the child learns to read and write. And yes, the child from birth is meaning-oriented, and this, too, can continue as she becomes literate. It's all well and good to say the child focuses on meaning but also learns form in the many contexts of communicatively purposeful, meaningful events. But how? How does the child learn this? It can't just be magic.

No, it isn't magic. Like the child's acquisition of oral language, it has much to do with collaboration and apprenticeship, to which we now turn.

CHAPTER 4

Collaboration

*What a child can do with assistance today she will be able to do by herself tomorrow." —*Lev Vygotsky, 1978, p. 87

This chapter focuses on the "with assistance" that Vygotsky speaks of: collaboration. It is about children moving into literacy in partnership with others. We begin by considering the nature of collaboration as it relates to early literacy, and then zero in on collaboration in children's writing (dictation) events and in their engagements with predictable books. The chapter ends with a consideration of familiar (memorized) texts as helpful partners for the young reader/writer.

COLLABORATION IN EARLY LITERACY

Vygotsky's words above may make you think of the conversations between 1½-year-old Jenna and Sarah and their mothers. In partnership, these mother–daughter pairs created conversations.

It seems paradoxical that these mothers engaged their daughters as actually *being* what they were *learning to be*: conversationalists. How can a child participate as a conversationalist when she isn't one yet? But what if Jenna's mother had said, "I'll wait until you know how to carry on a conversation and then I'll start having conversations with you." If she had done this, how could Jenna have ever become a conversationalist? Fortunately for Jenna, her mother has seen—and treated—Jenna as a conversational partner from the beginning, interpreting her body movements, vocalizations, and, eventually, words as relevant contributions to their conversation. Over time, Jenna takes on more of the conversational work; over time, she becomes a skilled conversationalist. Collaboration is an important factor in Jenna's oral language development, and it can contribute significantly to her literacy development, as well.

The features of collaboration that you saw in the mother–child conversations involving Jenna and Sarah also characterize literacy collaborations. The collaboration:

- Is often a bit ahead of the child—but not too far ahead. It "leans forward," as it were. It is in what Vygotsky (1978) called the child's "zone of proximal development" (p. 87), that is, the area where a child can function with the help of a more competent partner. This "zone" is neither totally beyond the child's reach, nor completely within her grasp. It is the area between the two, an area of promise and possibility.
- Often involves expert and novice(s)—an asymmetrical partnership. Together, they create something (e.g., a discussion, an oral or written narrative, a letter, a journal entry).
- Often fosters active engagement of the novice. The more competent partner tries to bring the novice into the process as fully as possible.
- Engages the novice in the very thing that she is learning. It is not an exercise, rehearsal, or drill, but rather the shared creation of a genuine conversation or a meaningful written text, or an interaction with an authentic text.
- Is sensitive to the novice, taking her into account and shaping toward her interests, her world, her competence level, her expressive ways.

These features of collaboration support the emergent reader and writer no less than the emergent conversationalist.

Emergent reader. Emergent writer. These are powerful labels, acknowledging two terribly important facts about the child's early engagement with printed material and writing implements: (1) it is real reading and writing, and (2) it is an early version of an ability that will develop further over time. This view of early readers and writers is fairly recent. It was only a few decades ago that adults believed that reading began with the pre-primer, the teacher's formal introduction of conventional print. We did not see it as reading when the 3-year-old picked up a familiar book and, while turning the pages, (re)told a story in expressive voice. We would not have seen Kelly's scribbles as writing—her invitation to her birthday party, her note to her grandfather. We might have found these incidents touching or amusing, but we would not have seen them as instances of reading and writing. Now we know better. We recognize that these young children are doing some things that accomplished readers and writers do.

- The expression in the 3-year-old's voice as she creates her story from the illustrated page tells us that she has entered the story. She is living in it.

- The story she (re)creates is meaningful and may preserve some features of narrative genre (e.g., in structure, in expressions such as "Once upon a time").
- She manages some of the mechanics of reading (e.g., holding the book right side up, paging front to back).
- Kelly's scribble writing conveys purposeful messages, holding them on the page, making them permanent on paper. That's what writing does.

We know that these early literate behaviors will, over time, become more refined, precise, diverse, and conventional, as happens in oral language development as well. And, as with oral language development, collaboration—enabling partnerships—can play an important role in fostering literacy development.

One can think of many collaborations within a classroom: child–child partnerships, small-group collaborations, one-on-one teacher–child collaborations, teacher–group collaborations (e.g., story read-aloud discussions or group text generation). However, in this chapter, I focus on two—dictation and predictable text—that reveal quite vividly the supportive nature of collaboration in the child's literacy development.

COLLABORATION IN WRITING: DICTATION

I have Buddy to thank for the children's reading response picture journals. Five-year-old Buddy (kindergarten) idolized his older brother, Brad (8 years old, 2nd grade), also a member of the class. Buddy insisted on doing whatever Brad did. Brad, an accomplished reader, loved *Captain Underpants* books by Dav Pilkey. So when Brad chose a *Captain Underpants* book, Buddy announced, "I want a *Captain Underpants* book." I gave him one and he carried it around for days. One day, Buddy overheard me talking with his brother about a reading response dialogue journal that he and I were starting. "*I* want a journal," Buddy insisted. "Sure," I said, wondering how I was going to engage in dialogue writing with this child who was just learning to write his name. And so began the reading response picture journal: five 6" × 7" unlined pages stapled into a wallpaper cover. On each page, the child (usually) draws a picture of a favorite book that we have read (as a class read-aloud or in our one-on-one reading in The Book Place), and then, working together in some way, we add written text. The journal is a kind of memory book. (Five pages seems to be the right amount for these children, allowing them to complete the journal before they leave, often with little or no advance warning.)

It's fascinating to see how different the collaboration is from child to child and sometimes even for different entries of a single child. The classic dictation event is child sitting beside adult, telling the adult what she wants to say, and the adult writing the child's words as the child watches, the adult sounding the words out as she writes, thereby slowing down the process and externalizing for the child's benefit what is—for the adult—an internal and automatic process. Yet that basic collaboration is very sensitive to child-in-the-moment. Writing involves so many things: generating ideas, selecting the words to express them, ordering the words in phrases and sentences, figuring out what letters to use to represent them, even going through the (sometimes quite arduous) physical task of forming the actual letters on paper. The collaboration we call "dictation" can shape itself to the child and her writing focus and effort at the moment:

> Donald draws a spaceship and then copies *Ahoy, Pirate Pete!* from the book cover (Sharratt, 2003). He then dictates "spaceship," which I write on a small piece of paper as I sound out the word. He copies the word onto the page. We read the page together several times as I point to the words he has written.

> After drawing her picture, Melanie dictates "The spider is spinning a web" (Carle, 1984). I sound out the words as I write them on a paper strip. This is a hefty amount of text for this child to write, so I give her a pencil and suggest, "Why don't you draw a circle around the words you want to write and I'll write the other ones?" She circles "is spinning a web," then copies them on her journal page after I write "The spider." We read the words together as I point to them. (See Figure 4.1.)

> Jay (6 years old, 1st grade) provides all the letters himself as he writes "Come back tomorrow," the dragon's words in *The Paper Bag Princess* (Munsch, 1980; see Figure 4.2)

> Tammy (6 years old, 1st grade) and Kenny write their own text, too, and my role is only to help them think—and talk—about what they want to write. Tammy writes, "Princess Elizabeth, Prince Ronald" (Munsch, 1980; see Figure 4.3). Kenny draws a picture of the two of us on The Book Place couch and then writes, "mye and mis Judy er reding *Officer Buckle*" (Rathman, 1996; see Figure 4.4).

Figure 4.1. Melanie's journal entry

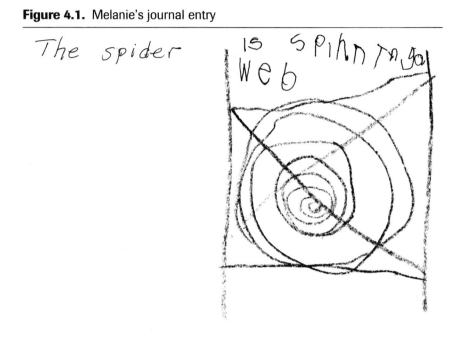

Figure 4.2. Jay's journal entry

Figure 4.3. Tammy's journal entry

Figure 4.4. Kenny's journal entry

Chad writes entries about Carle's *The Very Quiet Cricket* (Carle, 1990) and *Harry, the Dirty Dog* (Zion, 1956) on his own: "The verey quiet creckit was so quiet"; "Harry was a white dog with black spots who liked to do tricks. And liked to play." But a few days later, when he is writing an entry about *Something Might Happen* (Lester, 2003), his words come gushing out and I am just a scribe. It's not about the code now—no sounding out. Just writing his words quickly so we do not lose them: "Twitchly Fidget made up his own code that his friends already know—his code so they can come in any time and play tic tac toe."

Zoe (5 years old) loved the book *Dinnertime!* (Williams, 2001) especially the repeated refrain, "Run, fat rabbits, run, run, run/That fox wants to eat you, one by one." We have chorused our way through that refrain many times. One day, Zoe's entry—which she produces in a sing-song voice—is "I like rabbits, run, run, run/I don't know if the fox will come." She draws a rabbit picture and she and I share the writing task, with her writing the "I llik rabbits" and me writing the rest. She is delighted with her rhymed text. The next day, after we read *Goodnight, Moon* together (Brown, 1947), she writes in her journal, "Good night, good night/I don't know [if the fox will come] and eat the soup" (omitting the words in brackets). She goes into gales of laughter. She is on a roll now, and the next day her entry is, "Run, fat rabbits, run, run, run/[I don't] know [if the] worm [will] come and eat the cabbage." Her delight with the texts she was creating seemed to provide the momentum for her to carry out a challenging transcribing task. My role was only to help her remember what she wanted to write, and to be an appreciative audience, joining in her laughter.

Frank Smith, a psycholinguist and literacy researcher, once wrote an article called "Twelve Easy Ways to Make Learning to Read Difficult* (*and One Difficult Way to Make It Easy)" (1973). His "one . . . way to make it easy" is as true of learning to write as it is of learning to read. It is this: "Respond to what the child is trying to do" (p. 195). The examples above demonstrate the (potential) responsiveness of dictation. These children are all writing: They are moving from idea in the mind to its expression as words on paper. But this is not one act; it is many acts. A beginning writer may not be able to focus on all of them at once. As the child's focus and effort shift, so can the adult's response, whether providing a model to copy, demonstrating the encoding process, repeating the child's words—holding on to them so she doesn't forget them as she goes through the physical writing act—nudging toward the forging of letter/

sound connections, appreciating the child's product, and so on. Figuring out "what the child is trying to do" at a given moment is not easy. Often we get it wrong. But our chances of getting it right are never better than in one-on-one collaborative writing events. This child, this moment, this literate act: This supportive partnership.

COLLABORATION IN READING: PREDICTABLE BOOKS

"I just love *Gossie*" (Dunrea, 2002), Melanie (5 years old, kindergarten) tells me, hugging the book to her chest. And why wouldn't she love this book?! It's a small book (6" × 6") that fits comfortably in small hands. The simple, bright illustrations perfectly match the simple, bright text. Gossie, the "small, yellow gosling who likes to wear bright red boots," is an endearing character. The story is about friendship: Gossie loses her treasured boots and finally finds both the boots and a new friend when the boots turn up on the feet of Gertie, another gosling. What, after all, is more important to a 5-year-old than friendship? And then there is the text itself, a lilting, swaying sort of text. Gossie, the text tells us (in one sentence per page), is never without her bright red boots: "She wears them when she eats. She wears them when she sleeps. She wears them when she rides (illustration shows Gossie riding a pig). She wears them when she hides" (illustration shows a tree with a pair of red boots sticking out). Gossie also wears her bright red boots when she goes for walks: "She walks backward. She walks forward. She walks uphill. She walks downhill. She walks in the rain. She walks in the snow." There is repetition, too—not to the point of boredom, but as a satisfying refrain. No wonder Melanie loves *Gossie*.

Melanie also loves *Gossie* because she has made this text her own. It has been a gradual process. We began by sitting on The Book Place couch, Melanie seated on my right (important!), holding the book together while I read it aloud all the way through. The right-hand pages of this book hold the especially enabling text—the repeated refrains (e.g., "Every day"), and the second part of two-part pairs. The second time through, we could take turns (me reading the left-hand pages, Melanie reading the right-hand pages) and could read in chorus those pages that were less patterned. Melanie read "her" (right-hand) pages, but of course listened to "my" (left-hand) pages. Before long, she could read "my" pages, too, and I was able to remove myself from the collaboration. What had started as a three-way collaboration (*Gossie*, Melanie, and me) became a two-way partnership: Melanie and *Gossie*.

Did Melanie also love *Gossie* because this book enabled her to be a reader—a real one—competent, fluent, independent? I suspect so. The boost that this book gave to her confidence may have been no less than the boost it gave to her competence.

Recall the features of collaboration and consider these in relation to *Gossie*. This book is a bit *ahead* of the learner. Initially, Melanie could not have picked up this book and read it herself. But the predictable features of this text, coupled with the adult's support, placed *Gossie* in Melanie's "zone of proximal development"—her "reach range." Melanie's experience of *Gossie* brought together *expert* and *novice*—actually, two experts (text and adult), you could say. And both experts (adult and predictable text) fostered Melanie's *active participation as a real reader*. *Gossie* shaped to Melanie in many ways, but especially by drawing on her knowledge of language: the rhythms, rhymes, and tunes of the text; the two-part pairings; the story structure (baseline, problem, resolution)—all these features "stacked the deck" in Melanie's favor. For Melanie, *Gossie* was an important collaborative partner.

Predictable books like *Gossie* enable children to make good (sensible, meaningful) guesses as they read, and making good guesses in context is precisely what accomplished readers do. The words the novice comes up with may not exactly match those on the page, but the behavior—the process—she is engaging in is reading. Recall Maria looking at the words on a page in *Cookie's Week* (Ward, 1988) that says "On Wednesday, Cookie upset the trash can" and reading these words as "On Wednesday, Cookie bothered the trash can." Her sense of "upset" is different from mine in this context, but her reading behavior is very much like mine: She is making sense in an ongoing context.

Again, there are striking parallels with oral language development. The toddler also "reads" words in context. Margaret Donaldson (1979) offers this example:

> An English woman is in the company of an Arab woman and her two children, a boy of seven and a little girl of thirteen months who is just beginning to walk but is afraid to take more than a few steps without help. . . . The little girl walks to the English woman and back to her mother. Then she turns as if to start off in the direction of the English woman once again. But the latter now smiles, points to the boy and says: "Walk to your brother this time." . . . [T]he boy . . . holds out his arms. The baby smiles, changes direction and walks to her brother. (pp. 31–32)

The little girl does not understand the English woman's words, but she understands—"reads"—the context: the woman's pointing gesture, the brother's extended arms. You'll remember from Chapter 3 how mothers of very young children modify their talk so as to engage their children in conversation (e.g., by using short, simple sentences; by asking a lot of questions; by using special word forms; by using exaggerated stress and intonation; etc.). Recall that "motherese" also includes a heavy reliance on the immediately present physical context. When mothers talk with other adults, much of their talk is abstract, focusing on objects and events that are not present (e.g., movies they have seen, recent encounters with mutual friends, current events, trips they are planning to take). But their conversations with their 2-year-olds are very different, relying mainly on the shared immediate context. They talk about the toy the child is playing with, the food the child is eating, the clothes the child is wearing, the experience they are sharing at that moment. They are, in a sense, creating a supportive *context* (situation) as well as a supportive *text* (the words and combinations, the intonation and stress patterns, etc.) Both context and text are shaped to enhance the child's participation as a conversationalist.

Gossie (Dunrea, 2002) and other predictable books can support the developing reader in both the context and the text they offer. Contextual support often comes from illustrations that stay close to and visually represent the events expressed in the words. In some instances (e.g., *Rosie's Walk* [Hutchins, 1971]), the illustrations actually constitute the story line. The use of familiar story structure is another contextualizing feature that can help a child read the text. Think of *Gossie* with its familiar structure of baseline, problem, resolution. Often, predictable books draw on developing readers' world knowledge (e.g., the days of the week in *Cookie's Week* [Ward, 1988], the counting sequence in *Two Little Witches* [Ziefert & Taback, 1996], the animal sounds in *The Very Busy Spider* [Carle, 1984]). Illustrations, familiar story structure, and world knowledge are but three examples of features of a supportive context in which the words themselves are embedded.

Pattern is the crucial element of predictability in text, and you will remember from Chapter 1 how pattern-oriented young children are. We tend to think of "the 3 Rs" first: rhythm, rhyme, repetition—all three present in texts such as *I Went Walking* (Williams, 1989; "I went walking. What did you see? I saw a [color] [animal] looking at me.") or *Where is the Green Sheep?* (Fox, 2004; "Here is the [blue] sheep. And here is the [red] sheep. Here is the [bath] sheep. And here is the [bed] sheep. But where is the green sheep?"). In *Dinosaurs, Dinosaurs* (Barton, 1991), the repetition of sentence structures provides the pattern, without rhyme or precise rhythm, giving the text a more fluid and open-ended quality, while still offering support: "A long time ago there were dinosaurs. There were dinosaurs with [horns] and dinosaurs with [spikes]. There were dinosaurs with . . . and dinosaurs with . . .".

Perhaps most enabling of all when a developing reader comes to a book is her language expectation that words belong within the context in which they occur. Words and context fit together in written language, just as they do in talk. This fundamental understanding was enormously helpful to the child when she learned to talk (or sign). It can be helpful to her once again as she learns to read. Predictable texts build on this basic understanding.

THE IMPORTANCE OF FAMILIAR TEXTS IN LEARNING TO READ

There is nothing that makes a text more predictable than a child's familiarity with it. Think of the sing-song oral texts the child may already know when she first encounters them in print (e.g., *Five Little Monkeys Jumping on the Bed* [Christelow, 1989] or *Over in the Meadow* [Galdone, 1986; Langstaff, 1985]). And how about those favorite books a young child commits to memory, requesting the (accommodating) adult to read them over and over again, and correcting the adult's every minor "mistake"? How often we hear an adult say of a child's early reading of a favorite book, "Oh, she's not really reading it. She's just saying it from memory." *Just* saying it? "Just" is a dismissive word and diminishes the child's accomplishment. But even more, it fails to recognize the importance of familiar text for the developing reader. Once again, there is a counterpart in oral language development.

Language acquisition research documents the presence of "*formats* for interaction between mother and [young] child . . . 'expectable way[s]' of doing things together (Bruner, 1981, p. 44). Some early interactions become routinized. Typically, these are action routines with a verbal component: tickling games, peek-a-boo, action rhymes like pat-a-cake, patterned two-part exchanges such as:

Adult: Where's your [nose]?
Child: (points to appropriate body part)
Adult: (acknowledges child's action)

Adult: What does the [doggie] say?
Child: (makes appropriate sound)
Adult: (acknowledges child's sound)

In time, the child's language may include more extended "scripts" (Nelson & Gruendel, 1988) like Sarah's *Snow White* conversation (Chapter 1). It is assumed that the child's participation in these patterned language events helps her figure out how language works. Routinized discourse gives the child familiar material that she can "analyze"—not consciously, of course, but unconsciously, picking up on the patterns and beginning to use them in creating her own utterances. The situation seems analogous to that of written language. Memorized texts may become "scripts," serving as important material for the child to use in figuring out how written language works.

Think about this. If a child does not know the words of a written text, and also does not know how the encoding system works, then she has no way to begin to figure out the system. But if she knows what the words are that those little black marks encode, then she can possibly begin figuring out how those marks represent those words. The material becomes available for (unconscious) analysis. Classmates' names on cubbies provide such an opportunity, as do recurrent familiar written expressions like "I love you." And so do memorized texts.

Consider one final example. A 5-year-old is sitting on the floor of the den, a small room that adjoins the kitchen, where her parents are preparing dinner. The child is looking at a book of her mother's, a book she loves to look at, called *The Secret*. Each two-page spread has a beautiful black and white photograph on the right-hand page and a single Bible verse on the left-hand page. One picture shows a field of lilies and the accompanying verse is "Consider the lilies of the field. They toil not neither do they spin." Another picture is of a man tending a flock of sheep on a hillside, and the verse reads, "The Lord is my shepherd, I shall not want." The child knows all of the Bible verses by heart and can tell by each picture which verse is on the facing page. She has "read" this beloved book many times. But suddenly on this particular evening, she discovers that she can play a game with herself. She says to herself, "Find 'toil'." Then, pointing to each word as she goes, "Consider-the-lilies-of-the-field-they-toil. Toil! Toil! Mommy, Mommy, this one says 'toil', doesn't it?" She turns the page and says to herself, "Find 'shepherd'." Then, pointing as she goes, "The-Lord-is-my-shepherd. Shepherd! Shepherd! Mommy, this one is 'shepherd', isn't it?"

I was this 5-year-old child, and this scenario remains vivid in memory (my only memory of learning to read). I see now that this discovery about written language—that each cluster of letters matched a spoken word—was possible *only* because I already knew what the words on the page were.

There is a moral here: Celebrate the child's memorization of texts. And when she wants to read the same book over and over (and over and over!) again, believe that she has her own real reasons, even though you and she may not be able to say what they are.

If Jenna and Sarah are lucky, they will enter kindergarten and 1st-grade classrooms that invite them into enabling, collaborative partnerships including experiences such as doing dictation and reading predictable books. Because these literacy events are integrated with and build on the child's (oral) language knowledge, they provide comfortable entries into the world of print. And so the child embarks on a journey into literacy. Others will walk it with her.

Tomorrow, she will walk it on her own.

CHAPTER 5

Apprenticeship

Apprenticeship has two parts: (1) observing "experts" doing what you are trying to learn to do, and (2) performing, that is, actually trying to do it yourself as well as you can. In this chapter, we follow Kenny, a literacy apprentice (observer and performer) as he creates a story and an index. We also consider the children's books we use that support both sides of this apprenticeship—books that provide demonstrations for the child to observe, and books that offer invitations for the child to perform. Megan ends this chapter—Megan in a magic moment.

KENNY'S STORY

The morning read-aloud was *Miss Nelson Is Missing* (Allard & Marshall, 1977), a story in which a gentle 3rd-grade teacher (Miss Nelson) solves the problem of her students' rowdy behavior, by becoming "ill" and returning in disguise as a substitute teacher, Miss Viola Swamp, a teacher every bit as witchy as Miss Nelson is angelic. The witchy Miss Viola Swamp brings the terrified students' behavior into line, and they are delighted—and well behaved—when the kindly Miss Nelson returns following her "illness."

Later, when Kenny (6 years old, 1st grade) came to The Book Place to read with me, he brought a story he had written about his own "dragon teacher"—his own Miss Viola Swamp, as it were (see Figure 5.1).

This text doesn't only tell a story about a dragon teacher. It also tells a story about Kenny—Kenny, the writer. Clearly, Kenny is doing what writers do: creating and expressing their meanings using the forms available in their language system. Kenny is intent on telling his story here, a story closely patterned on the morning's read-aloud, which he found very engaging. His focus is on meaning; he necessarily uses (written) language forms to convey it. And his use of those forms tells so much about the system Kenny has constructed for conveying meaning in written symbols.

There are 45 words in Kenny's text (including numerals). Nineteen are spelled conventionally: *today*, *day*, *this*, *books*, *do*, *to*, *play*, *we*, *the* (4 instances),

Figure 5.1. Kenny's "Dragon Teacher" story

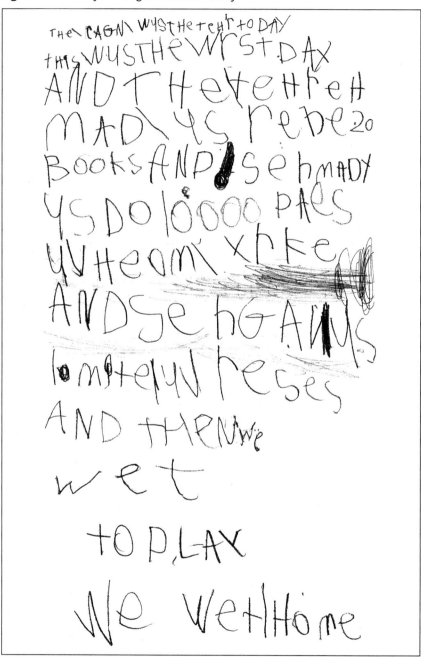

and (4 instances), *us* (3 instances). These words don't tell us much about how Kenny is figuring out the mechanics of writing—how to go from the idea in his mind to the marks on the paper that will communicate his idea to others. Looking at these words, we don't know how he came by these spellings. Was he relying on memory? On visual appearance? On letter-sound correspondences he has learned? On some combination of these, perhaps?

In contrast, Kenny's unconventional forms, his "invented spellings," reveal a great deal about how he is constructing the system of written language. As a toddler, Kenny had to figure out how meanings related to spoken symbols. Now he is figuring out how meanings relate to written symbols. And when he was a toddler, it was his unconventional forms (*comed, goed, mans, mouses*) that especially revealed his figuring out of that meaning-expression system—not just *what* he was learning, but *how*. His unconventional forms showed that he was observing many specific instances of spoken language, and from that array, he was identifying underlying patterns, regularities, and generalizations, and then using these in constructing his own original utterances. "Dragon Teacher" shows that Kenny is doing this again. This is good news, indeed, for it shows that Kenny is engaging in a *language* process, and as we know, language is what Kenny and all young children do best.

Kenny's text suggests that he is using a variety of strategies in constructing written language. Some of his invented spellings seem to rely on sound (i.e., his knowledge of the sounds that some letters represent: *wrst, mad, uv, gav, reses*). Some of his invented spellings seem to rely on his visual memory—how the written word looks. It's as if he is looking at what he is writing and saying to himself, "I know 'she' has an 'h' and an 's' and an 'e' in it, and I know there's gotta be an 'h' in 'teacher' for it to look right." And what about "wus"? If Kenny was only "sounding it out," we would expect "wuz." His spelling suggests that he may be relying on both sound and appearance. Is the final silent "e" in both "rebe [read]" and "heomyrke [homework]" the result of explicit instruction (silent "e" belongs at the end of a word)? Perhaps. You can see that initial and final consonant sounds are more salient to Kenny than medial sounds are: the "n" goes out in both "minutes [mite]" and "went [wet]," but the final "t" is retained in "went." When "n" is final (not medial), Kenny retains it: "dragon [dagn]." The "r" of "dragon" is lost, but the initial "r" is retained in "reses" and "rebe."

What Kenny *is not* doing here is as striking as what he *is* doing. He is not mindlessly imitating. He is using a model, but what he produces is not a carbon copy. It is a variation that reflects where he is in his processing of the written system. It is his variation, his re-creation in both his story and the forms he uses to tell it.

Does this sound familiar? It is what Kenny did when he learned to talk. He was an apprentice, patterning his own speech on that of the "experts" around him, but always with his own "twist"—expressing his own meanings in his own ways for his own purposes. And now, as he uses written language, he is an apprentice once again. He carries out two crucial actions, one internal, one external: (1) he observes, and (2) he performs. That is, he notices what "experts" do and he tries to do it himself.

KENNY'S APPRENTICESHIP

It is a given that one must be exposed to language (oral or written) in order to learn it. But exposure alone is not enough. Just being there while competent talkers and readers and writers around you do their thing will not result in language learning. The learner must actively observe what those others do. "Activity" is the crucial concept here. The learner's activity is mental and we do not see it, but we see the results of it. Kenny's earlier "comed" and "goed" revealed that the talk that Kenny heard around him was not just verbal noise to be imitated. Indeed, it is unlikely that he ever heard anyone say "comed" and "goed," and so his use of these forms could not have been imitations. Rather, the talk provided the verbal material that Kenny could mentally act upon to construct the complex system of meaning-expression relations used by his community. Clearly, Kenny is the same cognitive activist when he engages with print. And once again, we do not see his mental activity, but we see the results of it: *wus, seb, wet.*

As a developing writer, Kenny will sometimes copy the written forms he sees around him, and—like the children in Chapter 2 copying book titles in the sign-out book in The Book Place—he will copy in order to accomplish some communication purpose. (Children's early copied "I love you" is another example of copying in order to carry out purposeful communication.) But copying will not be Kenny's basic, driving process. In his unconventional forms, Kenny renders written language *as he has figured it out*, not as he is imitating it.

Written texts like Kenny's show why the simple dichotomy "right/ wrong" isn't helpful in understanding children's writing development. How could we label Kenny's forms as "wrong" when they are, developmentally, so *right*? These forms show him to be

- Observing instances of authentic, conventional writing;
- Deriving from those instances the underlying system;
- Trying out what he has learned—constructing a story using his knowledge;
- Incorporating knowledge of sound-symbol correspondences, the look of the print, memory, and explicit pointers; and
- Communicating his meaning in written form.

This is oh-so-right.

APPROXIMATION IN
ORAL AND WRITTEN LANGUAGE ACQUISITION

Think again of approximation. Examples abound in oral language of spoken forms the child uses that indicate her partial knowledge. Many of these show partial knowledge of word meanings. (The following examples are from Lindfors, 1987, pp. 160–161.)

A 4-year-old was trying to put on his shoes but could only find one of them. He asked his father, "Where is the other shoe that rhymes with this one?"

A grandmother found suspicious crayon marks on the wall while she was caring for her 3-year-old grandson. She said to him, "Oh, Chris. Look at this! How did this get here?" The child replied, "I did it, Grammy." His grandmother asked, "*You* did that?!" "Yes," he replied. "But it was an accident. I couldn't find a piece of paper."

One 4-year-old tells another, "That's dangerous. You know what 'dangerous' means? It means you might drop it."

Mother says to her 3-year-old daughter, "People are always telling you to 'share,' aren't they, Brenda? What does 'share' mean?" The child replies, "It means I get to play with somebody else's toys."

Other examples show the child's partial knowledge of word forms:

A 3-year-old, sitting in a booster chair, has finished her lunch and wants to get down from her chair. Unable to push her chair back from the table, she asks her mother, "Mommy, will you unpush me?"

A 4-year-old has been put to bed by a babysitter in her mother's evening absence. In the middle of the night, after her mother is at home and sleeping soundly, the child wakes her mother and requests to be put to bed properly: "I need to get goodnighted."

A 6-year-old is looking at Mercer Mayer's (1973) wordless book, *Bubble, Bubble.* He comes to the page where a fat mouse that had been blown with magic bubbles has suddenly disappeared. He points to the visual representation of the poof where the mouse had been and says, "It's a deblown mouse."

A 4-year-old tells his mother, "Robbers are real stealive."

A teacher asks a 4-year-old who is sweeping the floor of her nursery school room, "Are you mopping?" The child answers, "No, I'm brooming."

These forms are unconventional, certainly, but how could we call them "wrong"? No more could we call Kenny's unconventional written forms "wrong." Those forms show that Kenny, the writer, is a work in progress. They hint at where he has been and where he is going. It is as if we have stopped a video, capturing one particular moment in a continuous story. "Right" and "wrong" do not describe Kenny's process of becoming literate.

Neither do familiar, passive images of learning—the notion of the child as a blank slate to be written on, a lump of clay to be molded, an empty glass to be filled. Kenny's world (including his teachers) provides language experiences—lessons—of all sorts, some explicit, some implicit; some formal, some informal; some planned, some spontaneous. Kenny will tune in to some of these and ignore others. It's his tuning-in that fosters his language growth: his active observation of how the language around him is being used to communicate. There is nothing blank or empty or lumplike about this.

There are different ways to characterize approximation. Some educators call children's unconventional written forms "invented spelling," a label that captures the creative construction process evident in such forms. Invention, not imitation. Cyndy Hoffman (the K/1 teacher you met in Chapter 2) calls these forms "temporary spelling," legitimizing these forms as she talks with her children about the writing process they will go through.

Right away [at the beginning of the school year] I help [the children] realize that there are a number of different ways that are acceptable for them to write. In the language that is most widely used, I introduce stages of writing, from prewriting to conventional. . . . [I talk] to them about how they are *all* writers and they write in different ways and are at different places in this process. I tell them that some of the writing that happens only *they* will understand, and they will need to share it with us. And some of the writing that will happen in our classroom only *some* people can understand, and again they will need to share it. And some of the writing that happens, *everyone* will be able to understand, and that's what they're working toward. . . . [W]hat some people call "invented spelling" [I] call "temporary spelling" because [we] know that it doesn't last. And if we're reading something, [the children] can talk about, "This word is being spelled conventionally. It's written in conventional spelling." They know we have to go through stages like temporary spelling before we get to conventional spelling. I want them to know it's important to go through that. (Hoffman & Sharp, 1999, pp. 7, 8, 17, 18)

For me, the term *developmental form* works well as a label for these unconventional forms that reveal a child's knowledge of the writing system. *Developmental form* suggests two things that I believe to be true: (1) These forms suggest, rightly, that the child is progressing, and (2) over time, these forms will change. But this label does something more. For me, it brings together children's talk and reading and writing: overgeneralized forms in speech, miscues in reading, unconventional written forms—all these are instances of the same language process at work. All show the child as a language *apprentice*: observing, performing.

Let's take one more look at Kenny, the apprentice, this time as he creates what I eventually figured out was an index.

KENNY'S INDEX

The focal text is one Kenny wrote in his reading response journal. Unfortunately, I no longer have Kenny's actual text, but I do have my two journal entries relating to his creation of that text. These describe the emergence of this text (and of my awareness of what he was creating).

Entry 1

[When he came into the Book Place] I had [several books] ready for him, but abandoned those when he said (pointing), "There's the body book" [*My First Body Book* (Holtz, 1995)]. So I asked if he'd like to look at that and he said yes. We looked a little. He asked me to read the Contents and he picked a page/section (about growing up) that he wanted me to read.

We did and—as always—he had plenty to say (e.g., the need for practice as he had to do when he learned to ride his bike). . . . Since [his teacher] had told me he's interested in science now and enjoying doing experiments, we spread out some science books, browsed, and he took two.

Entry 2 (several days later)

I must learn to trust [Kenny]. Sometimes I can't figure out what track he's on (e.g., when he works in his picture journal or when he begins a *long* comment during read-aloud). But invariably he *is* on some sort of track that makes sense to him. If I just wait long enough and keep my mouth shut, his track/purpose/intention emerges. It happened today in The BP. We had read *Cookie's Week* (Ward, 1988). . . . He wanted to write—an unusual request for him. I got out about 8 books that he and I have read together in The BP (including *My First Body Book*) he had seemed to find very engaging. I asked which he was going to write about today—which he wanted to remember. "Cookie!" he said, with real enthusiasm. He drew his standard picture of the two of us sitting on the couch, and wrote, "me and Mes Judy." Part of the picture was yellow—colored with a crayon labeled "dandelion" [on the crayon wrapper]. He copied "dandelion" on the page. Then he went to the next page and took crayons one by one—very deliberate now—and copied the color name [from the wrapper] ("dandelion," "brown," "black," "cerulean") with a blotch (sample) of the color under it. Gray went on the next page [color blotch plus label].

Then he went to the next (final) page and asked me how to write "colors." I sounded it out with him. His intention was to write the number of the page where one would find the colors [i.e., the blotches he had provided with labels]. No page numbers. So he went back and numbered all the pages. Then he went on making an index [color name and page number where it was to be found in his journal]. We talked about Table of Contents and Index. He told me [what he had written] was a Table of Contents, but he couldn't put it at the beginning—he'd have to erase the whole book to have a first page where he could write it. I took *My First Body Book* and we compared Contents and Index—and figured his was an index.

But I wonder at what point he was deliberately making an index. He really does—and thinks—his own thing. I saw no connection between his copying color names and providing accompanying blotches [on the one hand], and the capturing of a book he'd like to remember [on the other hand]. And probably there was no connection. I'm not sure this journal has ever made sense to him—or, rather, not *my* kind of sense. (I'm sure it means something to him; I'm just not sure what). But his focus and attention were unmistakable and he put forth more focused effort on this—*his*—writing activity than I have ever seen him do.

Lesson here: *Trust* Kenny. Wait. Watch.

Kenny was passionate about information. His interest was intense, bordering on obsessive. Information books fed his hunger and he engaged with them wholeheartedly, one after another. He was fascinated with how information was organized in texts—how large bodies of information were made manageable. Just as Kenny had worked from a model text in creating "Dragon Teacher," so he did once again in creating his color index. Kenny, the apprentice:

- Observed authentic information texts; tuned in attentively to text features that were especially engaging to him; and then
- Performed—created his own text, modeled on the text structure he had observed.

Did Kenny come to his journal that day with a plan of making a color index? No. He started out in a way that he had before: "me and Mes Judy. . . ." But along the way, he apparently saw the possibility of creating a structure he found intriguing in the books he knew. (Who would have guessed that color names on crayon wrappers could have such potential!) His plan seemed to emerge from the work he was doing. (This is reminiscent of the 5-year-old, painting at the easel, who—when an adult asked, "What are you making?"—replied, "I don't know. I haven't drawed it yet.")

Notice how Kenny's creation of his index lived within a wonderful web of connections.

Talk and Writing. The reading and writing related to this event were suffused with talk: talk about tables of contents and indexes, talk about growing up, talk about what was written on the crayon wrappers.

Reading and Writing. As Kenny created his index, his writing and reading were so intertwined that it was virtually impossible to tell where the one ended and the other began. His writing stayed close to the model texts he read. He read the crayon labels, then copied them. He kept going back to check—(re)read—the pages he had written. He would write a page number, then go back and read the numbers from the beginning to be sure they were in sequence. Finally, he checked the accuracy of his index, reading each notation and checking back to see that it matched the journal page.

Observing and Performing. The two interacting parts of Kenny's apprenticeship were both in evidence and both inextricably entwined in this literacy event. He was clearly patterning his index on those he had observed in the information books he found so engaging; now he was performing—creating his version of that which he had observed. This combination—observe and perform—resulted in Kenny's unique creation.

Text and Context. Kenny's written text emerged from the situation itself—a journal and crayons and experience of past engagements with a variety of texts.

Within this complex physical and cognitive context, Kenny's index was born.

PROVIDING DEMONSTRATIONS AND
INVITATIONS FOR THE LITERACY APPRENTICE

If language-learning children are apprentices (observing and performing), then a fostering environment will be one that provides demonstrations (to observe) and invitations (to perform). The child from birth lives in a world of talk. There are demonstrations everywhere—competent conversationalists communicate with one another and with the child, and every communication event (a conversation, a story, a joke, a scolding, a verbal game) is a demonstration: This is how we do it. But not only are there demonstrations for the child to observe, there are also invitations. The child is invited into communication events as a participant. Jenna and Sarah come to mind as good examples; Kenny is another.

Looking at Kenny's dragon teacher story and his color index, you can sense the presence of demonstrations and invitations in his learning environment. Some were very close to Kenny's writing and seemed to be catalysts (e.g., *Miss Nelson Is Missing* [Allard & Marshall, 1977] and *My First Body Book* [Holtz, 1995] as demonstrations; his reading response journal as an invitation). But there were many, many more, because Kenny is in a classroom that offers abundant demonstrations and invitations into efferent and aesthetic engagement with a variety of texts.

Children are apprentices in their reading no less than in their writing. We choose some of the texts we use with developing readers and writers for their demonstration potential, others for their invitational potential. The first, "read-tos," especially support the observation part of apprenticeship; the second, "read-withs," especially support the performance part of apprenticeship.

Think of the read-tos first, those engaging texts that the child is unable to read on his own. Some are texts that invite an efferent stance, like *Tigress* (Dowson, 2004) or *Think of an Eel* (Wallace, 1993), both of which include two parallel lines of text—one narrative, the other expository. *Dinosaur Hunt* (Carr, 2002), an informational narrative constructed from dinosaur footprints near Fort Worth, Texas, is another example. Others invite the in-the-moment engagement of an aesthetic stance: *Honey . . . Honey . . . Lion!* (Brett, 2005), *Koala Lou* (Fox, 1988), or *The Recess Queen* (O'Neill, 2002), perhaps. These are texts we want to share with children, and so we read them aloud.

What is the demonstration here? At the very least:

- The purposes for which people write
- The sounds, rhythms, tunes of written language
- A variety of genres
- Concepts, ideas, and the words to express them
- A range of voices and literary styles
- The possibilities that texts offer—to wonder, to imagine, to predict, to inquire, to make connections to one's own experience, to empathize, to laugh, to visualize, to evaluate . . .

And there is always the underlying message: You will be this, too—an accomplished reader. No wonder read-tos are some of our own happiest early school memories.

Demonstration alone is not enough. One could not learn to play tennis by watching others do it. One must take the racket in hand and try it. It is not a tennis racket, but a book that the developing reader takes in hand in during read-withs. These are the texts we choose that support the performance side of the child's apprenticeship—predictable texts, Big Books in shared reading, song lyrics, texts that have become very familiar, and so on. The dinosaur enthusiast can't read *Dinosaur Hunt* (Carr, 2002) for himself, but (with help, perhaps) he can read *Dinosaurs, Dinosaurs* (Barton, 1991). In collaboration with another, the nature-lover can read *Insects* (Bernard, 1999), a book whose organizational structure and incredible photographs offer support. And children who are interested in different ways of being human in the world might, with a bit of help, enjoy *People* (Spier, 1980) or *A Country Far Away* (Gray, 1988). All are texts that invite an efferent reading.

Now think of the invitations that read-withs can offer for an aesthetic stance. These include invitations

- To chant along in a text like *The Three Little Pigs* (Marshall, 1989)
- To read along in a text like *Gossie* (Dunrea, 2002*)* or *I Went Walking* (Williams, 1989)
- To sing along in a text like *Over in the Meadow* (Langstaff, 1985), *There Was an Old Lady Who Swallowed a Fly* (Taback, 1997), or *I Know an Old Lady Who Swallowed a Pie* (Jackson, 1997)
- To move along in a text like *From Head to Toe* (Carle, 1997) or *The Little Old Lady Who Was Not Afraid of Anything* (Williams, 1986)
- To act along, taking parts in a text like *Have You Seen My Cat?* (Carle, nd), *The Shopping Basket* (Burningham, 1980), *Hi, Harry* (Waddell, 2003), or *There Is a Bird on Your Head!* (Willems, 2007)
- To laugh along in a text like *Blue Hat, Green Hat* (Boynton, 1995) or *Animals Should Definitely Not Wear Clothing* (Barrett, 1970)

And always, to discuss—to probe, to question, to wonder, to connect.

As we read a variety of texts to and with children, we discover that the observe/perform distinction blurs a bit. Yes, read-tos provide demonstrations that can foster observation. Yes, read-withs provide invitations that can support performance. But surely, the child's observation can also be actively engaged in read-withs. As he reads along, he may well be noticing aspects of print (letter forms, word spacing, initial consonants), aspects of narrative (story structure, motivations, plot, character), and aspects of language (rhythms, vocabulary, phrasing). And just as surely, the child's performance can be actively engaged in read-tos. Children (like ourselves) enter texts, vicariously living through the characters and contexts they find there. However, although the apprentice's observation and performance may occur together, by providing an abundance of both read-to and read-with experiences, we are thoughtfully, deliberately, tending to both parts of literacy apprenticeship.

MEGAN IN A MAGIC MOMENT

Megan (5 years old, kindergarten) liked to come to The Book Place. She enjoyed reading with me as we sat together on the couch. She also enjoyed writing in her reading response picture journal. The process was always the same: She would choose a book she wanted to write about, then she would choose a picture in the book and copy that onto her journal page, and, finally, she would copy the title of the book. All my gentle nudging to extend her writing was to no avail. I'd invite her into revisiting pages she had liked, casually flipping through the book, recalling parts of the text that she had found engaging when we had read the book together. "Oh, remember this part where . . . ?" or "Maybe you'd like to write something about this part that you liked." All for nothing. She would smile her sweet smile, and shake her head. Her three-step process remained fixed: (1) choose book, (2) copy picture, and (3) copy title.

One morning when I came into Megan's classroom before the children had arrived, her teacher came to me excitedly waving two of Megan's papers in her hand. On one paper, Megan had written the alphabet. What was striking was that her alphabet ended " W X Y N Z." On the second paper, Megan had drawn a picture and labeled the figure "C D" [Cedric]. Here, suddenly, was evidence of a beginning awareness of sound/symbol correspondence. This was a qualitative difference in Megan's writing. One day, copying letters on a page; the next day, selecting particular letters to convey a message—her message—that others could read. It was as if something had suddenly clicked in Megan's mind.

Such moments stop you in your tracks as you work with children! Where do they come from, these miracle moments? And why does the child's awareness arise at this particular moment? Nothing different seems to be happening in the learning environment—just another day, but suddenly there's that "click." How does it happen?

We can never know. That's the mystery that is the child's mind. But we can know, I believe, that such moments are most likely to occur in classrooms that support children's literacy apprenticeship by providing many demonstrations for the child to observe and many invitations for the child to perform. These will include opportunities for children

- To create their own authentic, meaningful written texts in collaboration with supportive adults and text models;
- To listen to (and vicariously enter) a range of read-to texts; and
- To engage in a variety of ways with a variety of read-with texts.

CHAPTER 6

Individuality

Every child is unique. It is a fact we need to take into account as we help children become literate. Trixie demonstrates this in a dramatic way at the beginning of this chapter. Then we move on to listen to other children's distinctive voices in their writing (books, reading response journals), in their engagement with illustration, and in their reading (book choices, responses). We'll see how two 6-year-olds—apparently new to the world of books—were able to quickly enter the literate, voice-full environment of their classroom. The chapter ends with a reminder of how joyful children's journeys into literacy can be.

A LESSON FROM TRIXIE

Trixie (5 years old, kindergarten) was a new arrival. I had met with her only once for a brief introduction to The Book Place, but even a brief encounter was enough to reveal a spritely child—tiny, dancey, smiley, talky—a vibrant, expressive little person.

I had tentatively planned for us to do the *Rosie's Walk* (Hutchins, 1971) make-the-text game the second time we met. This is an activity I use only occasionally, and very cautiously. It goes like this. The child and I read/talk/laugh/predict our way through this book (a great favorite), in which Rosie, a hen, goes for a walk, quite unaware of the stealthy fox following her. The fox is foiled time and again as he approaches Rosie with evil intent, and so she safely "[gets] home in time for dinner." The fox and his misadventures are pictured, but not mentioned, in the very simple, sparsely written text that tells only where Rosie is walking (illustration-only pages alternate with eight pages of print, most of these having only three words). The child typically enjoys predicting, from the illustrations, the problems the fox is about to encounter, then turning the pages to see if the predictions are realized.

After we enjoy the story together, the child gets to "tell the story another way," by arranging laminated, photocopied word cutouts to make matching text for each page (as many pages as the child is interested in doing). The word cutouts for each page are in a separate envelope. The child turns to a (text) page in the book, dumps out the word cutouts for that page, and arranges the words to match the printed text. Finally, we read the book again, and by now the child usually is able to read/tell the book pretty well on her own. I learn a lot as I watch a child do this. Some children pick up the words in any order and place each one under the word that visually matches it. Other children go left to right, saying each word as they go. And some children don't even look at the printed text until they have arranged the words on their own. Then they look at the print to confirm their arrangement.

You can see why I use this activity sparingly and proceed very cautiously. Like shared reading (Big Books), this activity could easily go from *story* to *exercise*. I have to be sure that it keeps on being another way to tell—and enjoy—the story of Rosie and the fox. But my hope is that the physical manipulation involved in this text engagement may help a child come to recognize WORDS as the building blocks of print. It's important that the reader eventually come to perceive the print on the page as words—separate "chunks" that match the spoken "chunks" so familiar to her in her own speech. Once again, there is a parallel with the child's oral language development. As an infant, the child is exposed to a continuous stream of verbal sounds. In time, every child comes to perceive this continuous stream as sequences of discrete units—separate words—and these become the building blocks of her own speech from the "one-word stage" on. Now, as an early reader, the child must perceive print not as a continuous black design against a white background, but as sequences of discrete units: words.

Trixie did not yet have the concept of text as separate words in one-to-one match with her spoken words. Because of this, because she was still young enough for physical movement to be an important mode of learning, because I thought this story would delight her, and because she seemed to be a reaching-out sort of person, eager for new experiences—because of all this—I thought Trixie would be a likely candidate for this *Rosie's Walk* engagement.

I couldn't have been more wrong!

We had begun by sharing several stories that Trixie had dictated to her teacher, who had then typed these and taped them into a bound book of blank pages that Trixie brought to The Book Place. Trixie had illustrated these stories. I read the stories aloud and we talked about them and about her illustrations. We moved on to *Rosie*. She became engaged with the story, though initially she was more engaged with her own birthday, still 3 months away. "My birthday is [date]. You need to write that down so you won't forget." (Unfortunately, I didn't—a missed opportunity on my part.) Trixie became more engaged with the story as we went along, predicting every misadventure that was to befall the fox.

"You can make this story yourself," I told her. "All the words." And so she did . . . for the first page. Then she looked at me and said, "This is really boring." So much for my sensible adult agenda!

"Well," I said cheerfully. "Then let's not do this. Let's do something else instead." And we did: We browsed the bookshelves, she selected a book, and we sat on the couch and read it together. My words were cheerful, but I kept wondering how I could have missed so completely, following an agenda that was totally at odds with hers.

We've heard so often that our teaching begins "where the child is." But surely it also must begin with *who* the child is—a unique composite of experiences, relationships, preferences, connections, ideas, understandings, expressive ways, and so on. In the above example, I didn't connect with Trixie not so much because I misjudged *where* Trixie was, but because I didn't take into account *who* Trixie was.

Working with young children can be so humbling. How often we get it wrong. Fortunately, we often get second chances. The next time Trixie came to The Book Place with me, she again brought her storybook from her classroom. We sat at a small table and looked at, talked about, and read her recent stories (pictures and dictated, typed text). Then I spread an array of "wallpaper books" in front of her (five plain 6" × 7" pages stapled in a wallpaper cover), and asked her if she'd like to make a little book to take home. Her face lit up. "Oh, I'll make a book for my little sister, Patti. She's 2 years old." I dumped out the tin of crayons and she took off. As she started her first picture, I said, "You can make the pictures and then tell me what you want to say about them and we can write that over here [facing page]." She replied, "This book is just gonna be pictures." (Oops!) I let it go and, after she finished her first page (a picture of herself and her little sister), she dictated her words for me to write down: "My baby sister is cute." She proceeded through the remaining pages:

- Picture of herself and a dog: "My poodle is cute."
- Picture of herself and a dog, clouds, and rain: "It is a wet night."
- Picture of herself in a bathing suit: "Me in the summertime and I am cute."
- Picture of herself with a happy smile: "This is a happy day."
- On the back side of the last page: "And we lived happily ever after."

We read her book together, and then she skipped and danced her way back to the classroom to read her book to the teacher who—as always with significant literacy moments—dropped what she was doing in order to focus all her attention on Trixie, listening intently, closeup, and responding enthusiastically to Trixie's reading, and promising Trixie that she would get to read her book to the class after lunch. It appears that Trixie will story her way into literacy, figuring out how print works by creating her own story texts.

We must be grateful for second chances. They abound in classrooms that are structured to invite individual choice and initiative, so each child can show us who she is and how she will—uniquely—enter the world of literacy. Then, when we miss, we can try again to provide invitations that are more appropriate for the particular child. This child; this self; this voice. This person who comes (in)to print.

WHAT IS "VOICE"?

Many scholars have focused on the notion of voice in written text. Though definitions of voice in writing vary, virtually all share the notion of the individual distinctiveness of the writing. It is suggested that the presence of the particular individual writer (the teller) is "heard" in her written text (the telling). There is an "imprint of individuality"—a "speaking personality"—in the written expression (Bakhtin, 1986, p. 75; 1981, p. 434).

An example from children's books might help. Think of the dinosaur books we use with our K/1 dinosaur enthusiasts. We would call the following four dinosaur books "information books," yet we hear a distinctive voice in each one:

- We hear a poetic voice in *Dinosaurs, Dinosaurs* (Barton, 1991): "A long time ago there were dinosaurs. There were dinosaurs with horns. . . . There were dinosaurs with long sharp claws. . . . Dinosaurs, dinosaurs, a long time ago."
- We hear a factual, "universal truth" voice in *An Alphabet of Dinosaurs* (Dodson, 1995): "Stegosaurus had triangular back plates, along with spikes on its tail, which probably served as good protection."
- We hear an inquiry voice in *T-Rex* (French, 2006): Walking through a T-rex exhibit with his grandfather, a child has many questions, but his grandfather has few answers. "Did he [T-rex] rip and tear as he charged and leapt . . . ?" "Maybe yes, or maybe

no—it was millions and millions of years ago. He MIGHT have leapt and lunged and ripped. . . ."
- We hear a storyteller voice in the created, realistic narrative *Dinosaur Hunt* (Carr, 2002): "Alone in the forest, the baby dinosaur looks around her world. . . . [She] is hungry once again, and her stomach growls. She spies a young pleurocoelus walking along a muddy stretch of land between the forest and the sea. . . ."

We hear a real person—the author's personal presence—speaking in a particular way in each text, expressing a distinctive stance, tone, and attitude toward subject.

As with the writing of published authors, so with our own: We inevitably bring our individual selves into our written communication with others, just as we do in our face-to-face conversations. Personality is multifaceted, and so we speak and write in different ways on different occasions. We speak differently to different partners (friend, grocery-store cashier, elderly aunt, student), in different events (party, breakfast with roommate or partner, parent–teacher conference), in different locations (church, library, classroom, living room), and so on. So, too, in our writing. The "voice" we use in a note on a birthday card to a close friend is different from the voice we use when we write a report about a child in our classroom, when we write a letter to the editor, or when we write a diary/journal entry. Our voice changes, but it is always present. We bring our *selves* into the communication.

Scholars have reached their conclusions about voice in writing mainly by examining adult-authored texts. But surely we hear the "speaking personality" in children's writing, too. Often, the child's written expression sings in our heads long after the writing is done.

VOICE IN EARLY WRITING OF BOOKS

How can children who are still new to expressing themselves in writing speak in this new mode in such distinctive ways when they write their own books?

Glen (7 years old, 2nd grade) writes about his favorite game and how to play it: "You can't tell anybody the password. You push the buttons and the little figures move around. . . ."

Fernando writes about his (and his friends') experience with a dog that sometimes visits his classroom (see Figure 6.1).

Figure 6.1. Excerpt from Fernando's book

Fernando and Glen are happy illustrating their books. Matt, however, will write, but he refuses to draw. He relies on photocopied pictures for his book, *Dinosaurs.*

Lakiesha isn't interested in drawing either, but she's very interested in family. In *Me and My Family,* she recalls shared family experiences:

I like tovisitmy
sisrtAnd my
nePhew
and Get to tok to
my cazns.
I love my sisrt
and my Brothr
and MoMandmy
Dad
We play Gems
MnoPoly and
We Wach mvs
and ~~wnt~~ wen
It snow
We mak
Snowman

One senses a unique self in each piece of writing. Voice: the "I am" in written expression.

VOICE IN EARLY WRITING
IN READING RESPONSE JOURNALS

The children's book writing is very open ended. Like all authors, the children choose their own topics. In contrast, the journal writing is more circumscribed, focusing specifically on books the child has read in The Book Place or during read-aloud in the classroom. Thus, you might expect the children's writing in their reading response journals to be more similar from child to child than the writing in their individually authored books. But it is not so. Even here, where children are (supposedly) "doing the same activity," distinctive voices emerge. The small journal with its five blank pages is a place for the child to record, in some way, favorite books we've read together that she would like to remember. Well . . . that's what

I think it is, anyway, though you already have seen how Kenny chose to use his journal to create an index. You also have seen Kenny's standard entry: "Me and Mes Judy. . . ." Other children, too, use this journal in distinctive ways, and the stylistic range among children is striking.

> For Buddy, some entries are pictures with labels: "This is the cat in the hat." (Seuss, 1957); "This is a brown bear." (Martin, 1995); or simply "Star Wars" (a picture and label having no counterpart in our reading at all). Other entries accompanying his pictures focus on actions: "He's making a mess." (*The Cat In the Hat,* [Seuss, 1957]); "This is Clifford running." (Bridwell, 1972).

> Megan, not one to take risks, typically copies a picture from the book and then copies the book title.

> Keniesha is a 5-year-old kindergartner. Most of her entries are dialogue. After we read *I Like Me!* (Carlson, 1990), she draws a cheerful pig waving and writes, "Hey friends." When we read Marshall's (1988) *Goldilocks and the Three Bears,* her entry is a picture of a girl (head only, apparently herself) addressing Goldilocks: "Hey Goldilocks. You wanna eat my soup for dinner?" Following our reading of *Red Riding Hood* (Marshall, 1987), Keniesha draws a fox and a girl's face (Red Riding Hood's? Her own?) and writes, "Oh my! There's a fox." And her entry for *The Ugly Duckling* (Pinkney, 1999) is a picture, bordered with leafy branches, of a swan swimming in water. Her text is, "I am so beautiful! I like the water."

The children's distinctive voices speak on each page.

USE OF ILLUSTRATIONS
IN EARLY READING AND WRITING

Eddie (6 years old, 1st grade) is looking at some books spread out in front of him on the rug in The Book Place. He is trying to decide which one to take with him. He picks up one, flips through it, and rejects it, tossing it aside as he says, "It has letters all over it. I can't even see it." The printed words that I see as the essence of the text, Eddie sees as interference. For me, the text is words; for Eddie, it is illustrations. His comment is a dramatic reminder that children often "read" illustrations, not just in books like *Rosie's Walk* (Hutchins, 1971) in which the crucial story action is in the pictures, but also in instances where the illustrations accompany the story line told in words. Well, for adults, the illustrations in books typically "accompany the story line told in words," but for Eddie, I wonder. He is amazingly attentive to illustrations in books, again and again noticing visual details I miss. On the last page of *Miss Nelson Is Missing* (Allard & Marshall, 1977), Eddie notices Miss Nelson's fake Viola-Swamp nose in a box on her bed. Halfway through our reading of *Blue Hat, Green Hat* (Boynton, 1995), he tells me, "They changed colors." He flips back a few pages and shows me that the character that had been wearing red is now wearing blue, the character that had been wearing green is now wearing yellow, and so on. And it is not only Eddie.

> Lashanda (6 years old, 1st grade) and I are reading *Ginger* (Voake, 1997). Ginger, the family's cat, has not taken kindly to the presence—and the playful teasing—of a newly acquired kitten. The last page of the book shows the two cats in a basket together, friends at last. Lashanda points to the picture of Ginger on the last page and says, "She's smiling"—a reading of the illustration that captures the new, friendly relationship between the two cats.

> Throughout *Dinnertime!* (Williams, 2001), as the fox tries to catch the rabbits "one by one," there is a scarecrow pictured in the background, never mentioned in the text. The scarecrow is not background to Eugene (7 years old, 1st grade). "He's alive," he tells me, pointing at the scarecrow. Eugene walks me through the book, page by page, showing me the scarecrow's changes in body position and direction of gaze (all of which I hadn't noticed, being so focused on the words).

> Alejandro and I are looking at the last page of *Silly Little Goose!* (Tafuri, 2001). The mother goose is leading a line of new goslings.
>
> *Alejandro:* She's taking the babies to swim.
> *JL:* Well, I'm not sure that geese can swim. I don't know if they have webbed feet like ducks do.
> *Alejandro:* They do. Look. (He points to the mother goose's feet in the picture, and indeed, they sure look like webbed feet.)

Illustrations can play an important role in children's early writing, too. It is well established that, for many children, drawing is an early form of writing (Dyson, 1989, 1993). However, when I sit with individual children as they write books and journal entries at the small table in The

Book Place, the drawing/writing connection becomes less clear. Yes, for some of the children, drawing supports their move into written words. And sometimes the drawing itself is all. As she works on a book she is writing, Zoe tells me, "This is gonna be one of those books that's just pictures." But then there's Randy, the ultimate dinosaur enthusiast, who (like Matt) will have nothing to do with drawing—actively resists it—though he's quite happy generating text to go with photocopied pictures of dinosaurs.

And then there's Howie (7 years old, 1st grade):

> Howie and I are in The Book Place. We read *From Head to Toe* (Carle, 1997). Howie's engagement is total. He leaps up from the couch to dramatize each animal. He crawls, he jumps, he thumps his chest, he claps his "flippers," he makes grunting noises and squeals. When we have read/ dramatized the book twice, he asks, "Can I make a book?" He chooses the wallpaper book he wants. He demurs about drawing, but with a bit of nudging, he begins. He completes four pages, with a simple line drawing on each page, and at the top "I am a" (which he is very proud to be able to write himself) and the name of an animal, copied from the book. He turns to the last page and at the top writes, "I am a donkey." The rest of the page is blank.
>
> *JL:* (gesturing to the blank space under his written sentence) I think you need a donkey here.
>
> *Howie:* It could be invisible.

Howie is happy with the writing, but drawing just isn't his thing.

VOICE IN EARLY READING: BOOK CHOICE AND RESPONSE

Just as children express their individuality in what they choose to write, so, too, do they express individuality in what they choose to read. (This assumes, of course, that children are familiar with different kinds of books and have freedom of choice.)

> Annette invariably chooses books about cats.

> Fernando rejects several dinosaur books in favor of *Fighters* (Stonehouse, 1999) because "I like books with lots of blood."

Lashanda has a particular book in mind. She wants the book "where the prince turns into a big ugly thing." (*Beauty and the Beast* [Brett, 1989])

Helen has a particular book in mind, too: "the ducky book" (*Silly Little Goose!* [Tafuri, 2001]) because "The ducky is funny."

Offered several versions of *Cinderella*, Ericka chooses one "because it's pink."

Malcolm (who is just learning to write his name) chooses a thick AMERI-CAN SISTERS book so he can look like an advanced reader and impress his classmates.

Hernando (7 years old, 1st grade) chooses encyclopedia-type books (books he can barely carry) because he loves to browse.

Even more striking, perhaps, are the individual voices we hear in children's responses to books. Even when children choose the same (type of) books, they respond to them uniquely. Luke, Randy, Trevor, and Winston are all dinosaur enthusiasts, but notice how differently they respond to dinosaur books:

For Luke, it's about blood and hurting, fighting and killing.

For Randy, the books are catalysts for the creation of his own eerie scenarios—stories with ominous presences. Weaving their way through each ghostly tale he creates around each book's illustrations are his two favorite dinosaurs: "Q-Rex" and "Jerk-o-saurus."

Trevor and Winston form a striking contrast, one a knower, the other an inquirer. Trevor and I sit on the couch in The Book Place time after time, always with a dinosaur book, and Trevor lectures. "You wanna know sumpin'?" he asks each time we turn to a new page. And this conversational move on his part "gives him the floor" to lecture to me about what's on the page. His knowledge of dinosaurs is staggering . . . and he is prepared to tell me all of it!

Winston is a browser. "Let's spread these dinosaur books out on the rug so we can look at them." He turns pages. Lingers. He creates scenarios for the illustrations, but, unlike Randy's, they are not eerie stories but stories of relationships. He lingers longest over a (movable) picture of a baby dinosaur emerging from an egg as its mother watches (Sabuda & Reinhart, 2005). He pulls the tab again and again to make the baby emerge. He looks at a picture of two identical dinosaurs sparring and asks, "Why are they fighting with each other if they're friends?" Often, he overrides my answer to his question with a more satisfying one of his own. One page shows a spread of different dinosaurs, in no activity or relationship. Or so I think. Winston sees it differently. "See, this dinosaur is the mom and this is the dad and these are the kids." He pauses. There is one dinosaur still to be accounted for. "And this is the aunt." And questions—always there are questions—wondering, probing, reflecting.

How can the interactions of four children with the same cluster of texts be so different? But think again. Maybe the question is, How could it be otherwise?

Read-alouds offer particularly striking demonstrations of individual responses to text. Children respond in a variety of ways. We find:

Personal Connections

Scott's mother has just had a new baby girl. He and I are reading *What Baby Wants* (Root, 1998), in which none of the adults in the extended family can soothe the new baby sister who is crying. It is the older brother who is able to comfort the distressed infant. Scott points to a picture of the older brother kissing the baby and squeals, "Just like me! That's just how I kiss my baby sister!"

The read-aloud is about a (mouse) child whose parents have given her the perfect name, Chrysanthemum (Henkes, 1991), but whose classmates tease her about having such a long name (13 letters) and being named after a flower. Wally says, "If I had a baby, I'd name her 'Bluebonnet.'"

Howie and I are reading *Mercy Watson to the Rescue* (DiCamillo, 2005). Mercy, the pig, likes nothing so well as hot buttered toast. And so, apparently, does Howie. He puts his hands together to show me "toast like this with cheese in the middle. When I wake up my Mom makes that for me."

Logical Connections

Gossie (Dunrea, 2002) is the book. Charlotte (6 years old, 1st grade) looks at the final page, where Gossie and her new friend Gertie are each wearing one of Gossie's precious "bright red boots," and says, "She [Gossie] knows how to share now 'cause if she doesn't she'll get two shoes-ez" (i.e., if she weren't sharing, she'd be wearing both boots).

Lance looks at a picture in *Blue Hat, Green Hat* (Boynton, 1995) in which the inept turkey has put socks on his hands: "Maybe he thought they were mittens." And on the last page, when the turkey has finally gotten it right—every item of clothing worn correctly—Lance says, "His mom must have dressed him" (i.e., he couldn't have gotten his clothes on correctly himself).

Predictions

Deshawna and I are reading *The Napping House* (Wood & Wood, 1984). The boy and the dog and the cat have, one by one, piled on top of the sleeping granny. As I'm about to turn the page, Deshawna points to the mouse in the picture and says, "He gon' be next. He gon' get on top."

When all the house-building efforts of the three little wolves have failed against the ravages of the big bad pig (*The Three Little Wolves and the Big Bad Pig*) (Trivizas, 1993) and they finally decide to make one last attempt—building a house of flowers—Keith predicts that the flower house will be camouflage.

Evaluations of Books

Marla says of *David Goes to School* (Shannon, 1999), "I love this book." "It's cool," she tells me several times when we read *The Very Busy Spider* (Carle, 1984).

Deshawna's review of *Bug Faces* (Murawski, 2000), an insect book we are looking at, is not so positive. "These bugs are yucky. I think I'm gonna throw up."

Evaluations of Characters

Ella Sarah in *Ella Sarah Gets Dressed* (Chodos-Irvine, 2003) keeps insisting on wearing an outlandish outfit. All her family members' suggestions of more appropriate attire just make her more adamant about her own choice. Mindy (6 years old, no prior schooling) comments, "She's a terrible two."

When Ronald, the bully in *Stand Tall, Molly Lou Mellon* (Lovell, 2001) finally—tentatively—approaches Molly Lou in a friendlier way, Kenny says of him, "He's changing. He's getting nicer."

Play with Language

As he lugs a huge dinosaur encyclopedia back to his classroom from The Book Place, Hernando tells me, "It *should* be heavy. It has dinosaurs in it!"

I read the title of the book Lance and I are going to read together: *The Shopping Basket* (Burningham, 1980). He laughs: "You mean a basket that shops all by itself?"

The morning's read-aloud is *The Araboolies of Liberty Street* (Swope, 1989). I get no farther than the title. "That sounds like Ara-*booties*," says Lance, much to the delight of his classmates.

Sensitivity to Language Itself

The text of the version of *The Little Mermaid* that Maxine (6 years old, kindergarten) has chosen for us to read together is rather difficult and dense, so I'm simplifying and paraphrasing as we go. She hears a difference between my language and book language. She complains, "You didn't *read* it. *Read* it."

Heidi (5 years old, kindergarten) and I are reading our way through *I Went Walking* (Williams, 1989): "I went walking. What did you see? I saw a black cat looking at me. I went walking. What did you see? I saw a brown horse looking at me," and so forth. Heidi says, "It sounds kinda like a song."

Inquiries

As we read *Caps for Sale* (Slobodkina, 1968), Chad wonders how the peddler puts the stack of caps on his head, given that his arms are much too short to reach up to the top of the growing stack and put another and yet another on top. (He concludes that he makes the stack on the ground and then, carefully, lifts the entire stack.)

Our reading of *The Very Busy Spider* (Carle, 1984) elicits some questions from Malcolm: "How do they have babies? What do they [the babies] look like?"

Some of the children's responses seem equally likely in the read-aloud and the one-to-one settings. But some are most likely to occur in the one-to-one adult–child encounter.

Extended Inquiry Sequences

Malcolm is very engaged when we read *The Little Old Lady Who Was Not Afraid of Anything* (Williams, 1986). It's the perfect Halloween story about a lady walking in the woods and encountering various clothing items (shirt, shoes, hat) that follow her home. Safe at last, she closes her door behind her, but opens when she hears a knock—the clothing items, of course, feeling dispirited because they are unable to frighten her. At her suggestion, the clothing items find a purpose at last: They assemble themselves into a scarecrow in the lady's cornfield. Malcolm has many questions.

"Why those shoes are walkin' for?"

"Why they scarin' her for?"

"Why was she in her rocking chair?"

"Why doesn't she hide upstairs?" [when there's a knock at the door]

"How do they [crows pictured on the last page] sneak in there to eat those vegetables?"

"It's gonna be a corn plant, isn't it?"

"Is she happy now?" (at the end)

And his final comment—though not in question form—has a puzzled quality: "But there's no hay inside him [the scarecrow]. Crows [i.e., scarecrows] have hay inside 'em."

Acting Out/Dramatizing

Howie (whose vigorous enactment of the animals in *From Head to Toe* you encountered earlier on page 86) impersonates pouty Beatrice (from *Beatrice Doesn't Want To* [Numeroff, 2004]) when he and I are in The Book Place together. He jumps off the couch, and says, "She go like this." Arms across his chest, he assumes a stubborn stance and angry face and says, "I don't want to do it! *You* do it!"

Time after time, Lashanda goes for the feel of the book we are reading. She jumps off the couch, saying, "Like this!" and proceeds to enact with her body whatever the characters are doing in the text.

We are looking at a dinosaur book. A T-rex and a triceratops are starting to fight, and I tell Wesley that the book says that sometimes one wins and sometimes the other does, but this time, the triceratops wins. Wesley jumps down from the couch so he can act this out. "Yeah," he says, jumping about while grabbing hold of his bottom. "He [triceratops] can poke his [the T-rex's] hiney [with his horns]."

Talking Directly to Book Characters

Renaldo (6 years old, kindergarten) and I are reading/looking at *Bug Faces* (Murawski, 2000) together. He holds the book up close to his face and asks the bug face in the picture, "Hey, you looking at me? What you lookin' at?"

Heidi talks directly to Mrs. McNosh in *Mrs. McNosh Hangs Up Her Wash* (Weeks, nd): "Hey, Mrs. McNosh, are you hangin' up your wash?"

Dennis talks to the gila monster in *Reptiles* (Spinelli, 1991): "Why you lookin' at me with your one eyeball?" He says to the marine iguana, "Ouch! Ouch! Don't touch me!"

In all these responses, children bring their individual selves into relationship with text. The children's presence resounds in their response to the texts they read, no less than the texts they write.

JAY AND MINDY: FIRST ENCOUNTERS WITH BOOKS

Jay and Mindy were both 6 years old and well into what should have been their 1st-grade year when they arrived. Neither had had prior school experience or significant book experience. The first time I met Jay and took him to The Book Place, he related to the books as if they were toddlers' busy box toys. Physical manipulation was all. He turned away from anything but pop-up books. "You got any more of these?" I spread some out on the rug where we were sitting. He barreled his way through them, one after another: open, turn page, pull tab, turn page, pull tab, turn-pull-turn-pull, toss it aside, grab the next, turn-pull-turn-pull. He didn't really look at what was on a page, but just made something move by pulling a tab.

Five days later, when Jay came to The Book Place, we began by reading *Ahoy, Pirate Pete!* (Sharratt, 2003), a book with a simple, limited story line and pages where the child selects (from six choices) and inserts cutout figures to complete the story. I was hoping this book could help him transition

from book-as-toy to book-as-book. Jay requested that we do the book a second time. We went on to *No, David!* (Shannon, 1998). There was laughter
here, and he asked to read it again. I reached for the third (final) book I had
selected: *Blue Hat, Green Hat* (Boynton, 1995), always a winner . . . but not
with Jay. I introduced the book and then said, "I'm going to read this book
to you and then you can read it to me." He pulled away, into himself, looked
down at the floor and said, "I can't read." "Well, I'll just read it to you," I
said. I did. No response. Then, as he was looking for a pop-up book to take
with him, this telling comment: "I don't like books much."

It was exactly 1 week later in The Book Place that Jay was treating
books as books. We began with *Once Upon a Time* (Sharratt, 2002)—a
book like *Ahoy, Pirate Pete!* with a simple, basic story line and cutouts for
the child to insert—then moved to *Blue Hat, Green Hat*. I read it to him
and he laughed out loud, but when I suggested that he read it to me, he
said he couldn't. "OK. I'll read it and you can do the 'oops' part." He did.
Then Jay started browsing through some pop-up books and flap books to
choose one to take with him, but now he started interacting with these as
books—message, language, and communication of meaning—not simply
as manipulative toys. "What's that?" he asked, pointing to an illustration.
"It's a porcupine." "Does it bite?"

Finally, 1 week later, we turned to *Blue Hat, Green Hat* again. I invited
Jay to read it. He took the book out of my hands and read it all the way
through, laughing as he went. When we returned to his classroom, book
in hand, the teacher dropped everything to focus entirely on him as he
read *Blue Hat* to us and we three laughed our way through the reading.
In the literate community of his classroom, with its abundant authentic
reading and writing invitations, Jay had found his way into the world of
books in just 3 weeks.

Like Jay, Mindy started with pop-ups and then moved to *Ahoy, Pirate
Pete!* (Sharratt, 2003) and *Once Upon a Time* (Sharratt, 2002), which she
wanted to do over and over again. What was most puzzling about Mindy was
her response—actually, her *lack* of response—during read-aloud in the classroom. She was a very practical, no-nonsense child who moved from activity
to activity during the day, with a sort of "OK. What's next?" approach. It is
an approach she brought to read-aloud. In spite of my (I thought) engaging
invitations to respond to (I thought) engaging books that I read aloud, she
just seemed to check them off on her to-do list: That's done, now what?

And then, one day, it happened. The morning's read-aloud was *It
Could Always Be Worse* (Zemach, 1976), a folktale in which a farmer goes
to the rabbi (or wise man) repeatedly, to complain about his house being too small to accommodate his extended family. Each time he comes,

the rabbi instructs the farmer to take more of his animals into the house, which, of course, becomes more and more crowded. Finally, the rabbi tells the farmer to take the animals out of his house, and the house is now quite large enough for the family.

Like all the children, Mindy was delighted with the naked baby pictured in an adult's arms on the cover. Mindy commented, "When I was a baby, I wore a diaper" (i.e., I didn't go naked). I started to read. I got as far as the man going to the rabbi for the first time and complaining because the members of his extended family "all live together in one small hut." Mindy, looking at the illustration, interrupted: "That isn't a small house. It's a big house." (She was right.) I read on, and more and more animals were coming into the house. Mindy said, "See, they could just take the animals out and put them in the shed and then they could clean the house and there would be enough room." I read on. The chickens, rooster, goose, and goat are all living in the house, and the frustrated farmer returns to the rabbi. The rabbi begins in the usual way: "Is it possible that you have a cow?" Mindy knows what is coming. She bursts out—impersonating the farmer—"*No!*" Then she speaks to the farmer: "Say 'No.'" Then she explains to the rest of us, "I'd say 'No, I don't have a cow.'"

How were Jay and Mindy able to move so rapidly into these authentic engagements with books? How were they able to bring their own selves into these engagements in a matter of weeks? Part of the answer is that they were being invited into many authentic literacy engagements in their classroom. But a large part of the answer must be that, however unfamiliar Jay and Mindy may have been with books, they were not unfamiliar with *language*, and they were in a setting in which written language was understood as and treated as *language*. There was (1) authenticity as children read and wrote real texts for real reasons; (2) a meaning-orientation toward written text as teacher and children discussed the variety of books they read; (3) abundant adult–child and child–child collaborations in a literate community; (4) opportunities for the children to be literacy apprentices: demonstrations for them to observe and invitations for them to perform. And it all floated on a sea of talk. In this literacy-rich setting, Jay and Mindy could find their own ways into written language.

THE UNIQUENESS OF EVERY CHILD

We find general similarities among children in the sequences and the processes of language acquisition, both oral and written. Some of these have been described briefly in earlier chapters. Knowledge of these general trends is helpful: It informs our practice as we interact with children who are becoming literate. But every bit as striking as the commonalities among children is the uniqueness of each child as she makes oral and written language her own. It is no coincidence that it is individual children and their individual stories and voices that fill these pages. This is the way of language development from birth. The stories that mothers tell are individual stories.

- "When you were little and you finished your lunch and wanted to get down from the table, you used to say, 'I all fin-shin.'"
- "We had a cat named 'Shadow' and you used to call every cat you'd see 'Shadow.'"
- "You used to ask over and over again, 'what dat?' You wanted to know the name of everything!"
- "When we went to the zoo, you wanted to see the 'nakes.' That's what you called snakes."
- "You used to love to be tickled. I'd be changing you, and I'd nuzzle all tickly in your tummy, and you'd laugh and then say ''gain.' You wanted me to do it over and over."

The stories are, inevitably, individual, for although every child proceeds as an apprentice, observing and performing as she moves through predictable stages, she does so in her own unique way. Each child creates language anew.

Mothers know this. Teachers do, too. If you ask a teacher to describe a child in her class, she does not give the verbal equivalent of a stick-figure drawing that could represent any child. No. She provides a rich portrait that could only be this particular child—his likes and dislikes, propensities, styles, relationships, past experiences, confidence level, family background, subject/activity preferences. It is not surprising then that each unique self that comes to the printed page will make sense of what she finds there in her own way.

JOY IN A LITERATE COMMUNITY

When I arrived at SafePlace, I had no idea how much the children would enjoy books. Bringing a child into The Book Place is like bringing her into a candy store—only better. In a candy store, she must select only a few items and pay for them; in The Book Place, every book is "hers" and there is no fee. Choosing a book to take back to the classroom often becomes a browsing time—and how these children do love to browse!

"What kind of book are you going to take today?" "Hmmmmm. A fairy-tale book" or maybe "A book about snakes!" And out come the books and we spread them on the rug and the child sits or lies down on the rug and browses—lingers over one book and then another; stops on one page, then skips to another; asks me a question about an illustration, so we read the accompanying text. Browsing is such a delicious luxury, as many adults know only too well—especially those of us who happily spend an hour in public library or bookstore just browsing. Do we give children enough time to browse? Yes, we want them to select books and read them all the way through, but don't we also want them to experience the luxury of browsing—to linger, to savor, to choose bits and pieces here and there?

After read-aloud in this classroom, it's time for the children to come with me one at a time to The Book Place. Hands go up. "Me! Me!" "Can I go first today?" The children realize, of course, that each one will have my undivided attention in The Book Place, and that may be a draw. But I think the real draw is the promise of engaging with books. The child knows that going to The *Book* Place is about books—reading them, writing them. *Books* are what they like. And not just for themselves, but also to share: "I'm gonna take this book for my Mom. She really likes cats." or "I'll take this truck book for my little brother."

Book Talk Time was another activity in which the children's love of books was stunning. This activity evolved in response to the (previous) teacher's request that I join the classroom to introduce the children to a variety of books. (I no longer do this with the children, as the current teacher weaves "book talks" throughout the day.) I would come to the classroom with my cart, which has six sections. In each section, I'd have books (six or so) of one type. One pocket always had "books that you can read yourself" (read-withs we had shared in The Book Place); and another always had "books I've read to you" (familiar books from read-aloud times, the read-tos). The remaining four pockets varied from one time to the next; for example, books about reptiles, fairy-tale books, counting/math books (Wahl, 1985; Schwartz, 1985), books about the body, books by a favorite author (Shannon, Carle), wordless books, and dinosaur books. The bottom of the cart held carpet squares. I would introduce the books briefly, telling the children what types of books were in the pockets, and showing/talking about a few specific books. Then I'd call the children to come one or two at a time to choose a book (or two) and a carpet square ("Your magic carpet"), and then they would find a place in the room to sit and enjoy the book(s). We ended Book Talk Time by coming together on the rug for a sharing time. I was thinking of this activity as a way into DEAR time/SSR (Drop Everything and Read/Sustained Silent Reading), hoping to gradually extend the children's book-engagement time. It didn't work out quite as I expected. Yes, the children did become engaged with their books, and, yes, the engagement time did increase slightly, but the children reshaped this activity as a more social event than I had intended. After 8 minutes or so, they would begin to scoot their carpet squares together so they could share their books with each other. But what was so stunning was their reactions when I would introduce the books initially. The children would positively salivate! "Ooo Ooo Ooo! I want that one." "Oh, I'm gonna take that one." "Miss! Miss! Can I have that one?" "Save that one for me, pleeeeeeeze!" (Talk about candy in a candy store!) They could not wait to be called to select a book. And I ask myself, Where did we get the idea that we have to "motivate" young children to engage with books by giving rewards, prizes, or stars on a chart? *Books* are the reward. The children in this classroom had all been there only a few weeks (always the case at SafePlace), but the adults only needed to provide

- Time to explore books
- Places to explore books (e.g., book corner; home)
- Books to explore (a variety of accessible books in The Book Place and an abundance—frequently changed—in the book corner in the classroom)
- Demonstrations of exploring books—e.g., a variety of genres presented in read-alouds or the sharing of Big Books; many books used in Math and Science
- Choice of *what* to read (e.g., a variety of genres and subjects) and also of *how* to read (e.g., alone, with a friend, browsing, following along at the listening station)
- Sharing opportunities—e.g., a book going home every day to share with family, books getting shared with friends in the classroom or with the children's "reading buddies" in the daycare classrooms
- Response opportunities—to write, to talk, to draw

The adults provided; the children did the rest. They simply loved books.
All but Conrad.
Conrad (7 years old, 2nd grade) had had 1-plus year of schooling in some sort of school/program for gifted children. For Conrad, books had only to do with assignments, points, grades, credits, merits, and demerits. It was all about how much and how many, about more than and less than: What's the number of pages in this book? This book is harder/easier or longer/shorter than that one. I've read more books than

you have. Conrad's mother shared her son's orientation. The first day Conrad was in this classroom, he took a book home, as all the children did every day. The next day before school, his mother asked the teacher, "How many pages does he have to read every night?" I'm not sure what she made of the teacher's explanation that the purpose was that Conrad would enjoy reading the book and perhaps share it with her.

Where had the joy of books gone for this child? It was there for all the others. Why did he engage with books only as a chore, never as a pleasure? I have to believe that the adults in Conrad's life bear some responsibility for this.

Children acquiring oral language do not approach this learning as a chore. It is not about points or grades, competition or prizes.

- It is about connection with others.
- It is about exploration of the world.
- It is about expression of feelings.

The momentum comes from within us—the social, intellectual, emotional beings we are. Conrad's reading behavior suggests that we can disrupt this momentum when the child comes to written language, that we can derail the child onto a joyless track. But why would we want to do this?

Our best hope is surely to support children's language ways into literacy: authenticity, meaning-orientation, collaboration, apprenticeship, individuality.

And joy.

Appendix

The problem of domestic violence in America is huge. One study reports that "nearly one-third (31%) of American women report being physically or sexually abused by an intimate partner at some point in their lives." (Wilson, 2006, p. 8) And often, there are children watching: "As many as 3.3 million to 10 million children in the United States are at risk for exposure to domestic violence" (Wilson, 2006, p. 34).

Wilson (2006) calls domestic violence "truly equal opportunity," for it "crosses all socioeconomic, ethnic, racial, educational, age, and religious lines" (p. 15). The image of domestic violence that comes to mind first may be the woman with black eyes and bruises, but physical violence is only one type of abuse. Wilson (2006) defines *abuse* as "any repeated attempts to control, manipulate, or demean another individual using physical, emotional, or sexual tactics" (p. 9). Thus, the domestic violence that many children witness includes not only physical control (e.g., hitting, shoving, choking, arm-twisting), but also manipulation through emotional means (e.g., insulting, threatening, humiliating, criticizing, ridiculing) and sexual means (e.g., forcing unwanted and/or hurtful intimate acts).

If you are a teacher, it is inevitable that you will teach children who are living in situations of domestic violence. Over the past several decades, we have become increasingly aware of child abuse—how to recognize the signs, what to do about it, our legal responsibility with respect to this abuse. But there are often serious consequences for children who are exposed to violence in their homes, even if they are not being abused themselves. I asked Barri Rosenbluth (school-based services director at SafePlace) and Tracy Alvarez (school-based counselor at SafePlace) how a teacher can recognize signs that a student in her classroom may be living with domestic violence, and how she can respond to that child in a helpful way. Here is our conversation.

JL: How might a kindergarten or 1st-grade teacher recognize
behavioral indications that a child may be dealing with—watching,
experiencing—domestic violence at home? What might a teacher see?

TA: I think every child reacts in a different way, but aggression is one thing a teacher might notice, especially because young children aren't as verbal. They're more likely to express things behaviorally. Another indication is difficulty concentrating on school work, or excessive absences. The child might be hypervigilant, wondering: Is it going to be safe here?

BR: Sometimes children living with domestic violence appear to be neglected, and so there might not be these other overt symptoms of aggression or what Tracy just talked about, but it could just be that you notice the child's wearing the same clothes for 3 days. Or the child maybe has an injury or cut or something that hasn't been tended to. So it could be little things that might not immediately pop out as domestic violence but just neglect because the parents are focused on other things. Also you might notice the child falling asleep in class because he/she was up late, the child doesn't have a regular bedtime, or maybe there was fighting that kept him/her up.

TA: Sometimes children don't understand why their parents are fighting, so they might think they caused it in some way. You might find them trying extra hard in school, trying to be the perfect child: If I don't do anything to upset the home then maybe the fighting will stop.

JL: Are there differences between boys and girls?

TA: It differs for every child, but I think that more often girls deal with the trauma inwardly. They might be withdrawn, quiet, or depressed and not have as much social interaction with their peers, whereas boys might be more aggressive.

BR: You would want to notice any kind of problems with peer relationships. Of course, all these things we're saying could be signs of any number of problems, not just exposure to domestic violence. But I think the main point here is that you should always include the possibility that domestic violence is a part of the picture. With children who don't have good relationship skills—they're either the target of a lot of bullying, or they're the perpetrator of a lot of bullying, or they're socially isolated because they don't know how to make friends or keep friends—sometimes the problem is that they're not learning those skills at home.

TA: Maybe there is not violence going on at home, but if they're moving from place to place to escape the violence, they may have problems adjusting to school.

BR: And you may see a lack of trusting other people. And that can manifest in so many ways. Perhaps the child has had to move a lot, or maybe the child's parents have said, "Don't talk to anybody about what you saw or about what happened." So there's going to be a lack of trust.

JL: I would think the child might partly have difficulty building friendships because he can't bring another child home or go over to the another child's house.

BR: Right. Or attend sleep-overs or all of the things that you do with friends that cement those relationships.

JL: What might the teacher do if she sees behavior for which she thinks domestic violence at home might be *a* cause, if not *the* cause? Tracy, how does a teacher effectively respond?

TA: I think the first thing is to recognize that it's not something that's easy to talk about, and that (like Barri was saying) the child might very well have been told, "You can't say anything about this. Don't tell anybody about what's going on at home." So there may be the fear that, if they do tell, there will be negative consequences. But if they decide to start talking about their experience, it is important to believe the child and listen to the child without interrupting. Let them know, in a very comforting, nonjudgmental way, that you realize how hard it must have been for them to come forward and talk about their experience.

JL: Is there anything that the teacher can do to encourage the child to speak up?

TA: Well, maybe checking on the student's behaviors, like if they're falling asleep in class—noticing those behaviors and saying, "I've noticed you've been falling asleep in the morning. Is there anything going on that's not letting you sleep at home?" So maybe not being so direct, but noticing when the child is having a hard time at school and commenting on the behavior.

BR: I would also encourage teachers to try to create a private space for doing this. It's so easy in the classroom to not be thinking about privacy because there is none. Try to talk with the child at a time when there aren't other students around. Students can be very aware—even young kids—that other people are listening, and they're not going to feel comfortable talking.

TA: It's important to let them know they are not in trouble in any way. Often, when you ask a child to come in to talk to you, they might fear that "Oh, I did something wrong." So starting off by saying, "You're not in any trouble" and just really putting them at ease before you start that conversation.

JL: What does the teacher do about the parents? And in her interaction with parents?

TA: I think it's important to get other school officials involved that can maybe address that better—social workers, school psychologists, counselors—professionals who might know more about the resources available for the parents.

BR: And teachers might be afraid about talking to parents about this. Maybe they don't know if it's going to bring negative consequences to the child or if they're legally allowed to talk to the parents about this. They know it's going to create difficult relationships if they bring this up.

JL: So in parent–teacher conferences the teacher would just stay right with the child's academics and social behavior: "This is what I'm seeing going on in the classroom."

TA: Absolutely, bring up the behavior: "I notice that your child has been falling asleep in class"—specifically, the behaviors that are affecting their academic performance.

BR: I think that if the teacher is concerned, she might make a referral or say, "Would you be willing to meet with a counselor?" I would guess that most parents are not going to want to discuss this with the teacher because they probably feel like it will affect how the teacher reacts to their child. They might feel more comfortable with a counselor.

JL: Would it be appropriate for the teacher to say something like, "I notice that Jeremy seems to be kind of tired—seems to be having difficulty staying awake"?

BR: Right. "What can you tell me about that?" I would say if the parent brings it up on their own—"We're having some trouble at home"—maybe that's the opportunity for the teacher to say, "Well, I'm concerned about him."

JL: "And perhaps we can get some help with this."

BR: Yes.

JL: And here the teacher can move into suggesting a referral.

BR: Yes. I like that approach and letting the parent bring it up if she wishes to. Then the teacher really should be prepared to know who to get—who could be called for help. It would be great if the teacher said, for example, "Well have you heard of SafePlace?" But they could also just go to the school counselor or school social worker.

TA: And I think it's important, too, for the teacher not to make promises to the student that they can't follow through on, like, "I promise that this is never going to happen again." Sometimes you want to protect the child and keep the child safe, but a lot of that is out of your control, so just let them know that you're available to be supportive and to listen and to help them get the services that they need, but don't pretend that you're going to solve the problem or that things are going to be better tomorrow.

JL: I'm trying to think of some things that you say to children. Do you say something like, "I'm sorry that you're having a problem at home"? What do you say?

TA: "It's not your fault."

JL: And you say, "Sometimes children think it's their fault, but it isn't."

TA: Yes. And you try to normalize the feelings that they're having: "It must be really scary for you. It must be really frustrating. You must feel very angry." And you let them know that those feelings are all completely normal for them to have. And that they're not alone. It can be very isolating. Let them know that they're not the only ones who are going through this experience, that there are other children. And there are resources for children.

BR: I think that sometimes adults do react like, "Oh, I've got to save this child's life right now." We know from experience that children typically stay with their families even if there has been lots of abuse, and they have relationships with their families, and it could scare them to think about not having those relationships and somebody not being in their life. We can't assume that they want the perpetrator out of the house or that they are afraid or that they're angry. I think we have to really let them tell us how they feel. We should ask, "How are you feeling about this?", and "What can I do to help?", and "What would you like me to do?" And maybe they say, "I don't know." But maybe they do say, "I want you talk to my Mom, I want you to talk to my Dad, I want you to make them stop, I want you to call the police." But I think we have to ask.

TA: It's hard to hear stories from children, and it's important, I think, to try not to react too emotionally. Follow the lead of the child. Ask, "How are you feeling about this?"

BR: I think it's really helpful to the parent for the teacher to talk, in the parent conference, about the child's relationships with other children if the teacher has any concern about that. I think that the parent needs feedback from the teacher about how what may be going on at home is affecting them at school, because a lot of times parents can feel like, "Well, my child's not witnessing it so they're not being affected by it. They're not the victim themselves, so they're not getting hurt by it." They can downplay it, but if the teacher can say, "You know, Joey has a lot of trouble getting along with his peers. He really has a bad temper, and I see him throwing things" or "Other children are afraid of him"—parents need to hear that.

JL: I was thinking that with very young children—K/1, age 5/6—you might get expressions of the home situation in things that children draw or writing that they dictate.

TA: Definitely in play they might act out the problems going on at home.

BR: What do you see?

TA: Sometimes just with the horse family—they're pretending they're horses and the mom and dad will be fighting or the mom will be yelling at the child or you know just acting out what's going on at home through—

BR: Horses. (Laughter)

TA: Yes. Through their play.

JL: Let's think about resources for the teacher. Now, supposing the teacher has identified the behavior and she's a little suspicious and she's responding in all these sensitive ways. She wants to get more help. Where does she go?

TA: I've written a list of some resources that I think would be helpful. [See below.] I've included an overview and a manual and some case studies in which children actually talk about their experiences. Also several books for children—for reading to the child or just to read yourself and see "How do I talk about domestic violence with a child?"

BR: I would want every teacher to know their local domestic violence center phone number. Or the national domestic violence hotline. This one you can call from anywhere in the country. It's an 800 number. So if the teacher is in a small community that doesn't have a local center, she should call the national hotline, which will patch her through to the nearest shelter.

TA: And I think teachers should find out what resources are available locally. Use the resources that you have on campus to get more information for outside resources.

Melinda Cantu, shelter director of SafePlace (Austin, TX) tells us, "Children who live in homes where there is family violence live in fear, confusion, and pain. A lot of our work [at the shelter] is to help create a sense of safety for these children—safety to express themselves, safety to be themselves, and safety from abuse and fear." (Wilson, 2006, p. 32) She is describing a domestic violence shelter, but she could be describing a classroom—a safe place for children to be, to interact, to learn, to grow.

TRACY'S SUGGESTED RESOURCES

Resources Available for Teachers Online

Children Exposed to Domestic Violence: A Teacher's Handbook to Increase Understanding and Improve Community Responses. London, Ontario: Centre for Children & Families in the Justice System, London Family Court Clinic. http://www.lfcc.on.ca/teacher-us.pdf

Teacher's Resource: Child Abuse and Domestic Violence Readings from Childhood and Education. Published by the Association for Childhood Education International. http://www.acei.org/TR%20Child%20Abuse.pdf

What about Me? Seeking to Understand a Child's View of Violence in the Family. London, Ontario: Centre for Children & Families in the Justice System, London Family Court Clinic. http://www.lfcc.on.ca/what about me.pdf

Books for Children

(The following descriptions come from amazon.com.)

Bernstein, S. C., & Ritz, K. (1991) *A family that fights.* Morton Grove, IL: A. Whitman. Henry's parents fight often and his father sometimes hits his mother, causing Henry to feel frightened and ashamed. The book includes a list of things children can do in situations of family violence.

Hochban, T. (1994). *Hear my roar: A story of family violence.* Buffalo, NY: Firefly Books. This story is told in the form of an allegory featuring a family of bears. This child-centered look at family violence encourages victims to take action to help break the cycle of abuse.

Trottier, M. (1997). *A safe place.* Morton Grove, IL: A. Whitman. This is a book about Emily and her mother as they escape to a shelter for abused women and children. . . . Trottier acknowledges Emily's complicated feelings of guilt, displacement, and concern for her father . . . [and describes Emily's] relief of living in a place where there is no danger or anger, a place where her mother can relax and smile.

Further Reading

Language Structure and Acquisition

Crystal, D. (2006). *How language works: How babies babble, words change meaning, and languages live or die.* New York: The Overlook Press.

Fromkin, V., Rodman, R., & Hyams, N. (2006). *An introduction to language* (8th ed.). Boston: Heinle.

Golinkoff, R., & Hirsh-Pasek, K. (2000). *How babies talk: The magic and mystery of language in the first three years of life.* New York: Penguin (A Plume Book).

Power, B. M., & Hubbard, R. S. (2002). *Language development: A reader for teachers* (2nd ed.). Upper Saddle River, NJ: Merrill Prentice Hall.

Language and Culture

Heath, S. B. (1983). *Ways with words: Language, life, and work in communities and classrooms.* New York: Cambridge University Press.

Early Literacy

Clay, M. M. (1998). *By different paths to common outcomes.* York, ME: Stenhouse.

Dyson, A. H. (1989). *Multiple worlds of child writers: Friends learning to write.* New York: Teachers College Press.

Dyson, A. H. (1993). *Social worlds of children learning to write in an urban primary school.* New York: Teachers College Press.

Dyson, A. H. (1997). *Writing superheroes: Contemporary childhood, popular culture, and classroom literacy.* New York: Teachers College Press.

Edelsky, C. (2006). "Literacy: Some purposeful distinctions." In *With literacy and justice for all: Rethinking the social in language and education.* Mahwah, NJ: Lawrence Erlbaum.

Goodman, Y., & Martens, P. (2007). *Critical issues in early literacy: Research and pedagogy.* Mahwah, NJ: Lawrence Erlbaum.

Classroom Talk

Cazden, C. B. (2001). *Classroom discourse: The language of teaching and learning.* Portsmouth, NH: Heinemann.

Gallas, K. (1995). *Talking their way into science: Hearing children's questions and theories, responding with curricula.* New York: Teachers College Press.

Johnston, P. H. (2004). *Choice words: How our language affects children's learning*. Portland, ME: Stenhouse.

Paley, V. G. (1997). *The girl with the brown crayon*. Cambridge, MA: Harvard University Press.

Paley, V. G. (1981). *Wally's stories*. Cambridge, MA: Harvard University Press.

Life in Vibrant Classrooms

Avery, C. (2002). *. . . And with a light touch: Learning about reading, writing, and teaching with first graders*. Portsmouth, NH: Heinemann.

Fisher, B. (1998). *Joyful learning in kindergarten*. Portsmouth, NH: Heinemann.

King, R. (1999). Letters home. In J. W. Lindfors & S. J. Townsend (Eds.), *Teachers' voices: Language arts*. Urbana, IL: National Council of Teachers of English.

Seifert, P. (1999). Inquiry in the kindergarten. In J. W. Lindfors & S. J. Townsend (Eds.), *Teachers voices: Language arts*. Urbana, IL: National Council of Teachers of English.

Children's Literature

Norton, D. E. (2006). *Through the eyes of a Child: An introduction to children's literature* (7th ed.). Upper Saddle River, NJ: Merill Prentice Hall.

Sipe, L. R. (2008). *Storytime: Young children's literary understanding in the classroom*. New York: Teachers College Press.

Domestic Violence

Wilson, K. J. (2006). *When violence begins at home: A comprehensive guide to understanding and ending domestic abuse*. Alameda, CA: Hunter House Publishers.

References

Allard, H., & Marshall, J. (1977). *Miss Nelson is missing*. Boston: Houghton Mifflin.

Avery, C. (2002). . . . And with a light touch: Learning about reading, writing and teaching with first graders. Portsmouth, NH: Heinemann.

Bakhtin, M. M. (1981). *The dialogic imagination*. Austin: The University of Texas Press.

Bakhtin, M. M. (1986). *Speech genres & other late essays*. Austin: The University of Texas Press.

Barrett, J. (1970) *Animals should definitely not wear clothing*. New York: Atheneum Books for Young Readers.

Barton, B. (1991). *Dinosaurs, dinosaurs*. New York: Trophy, HarperCollins.

Bernard, R. (1999). *Insects*. New York: National Geographic.

Bishop, C. H., & Wiese, K. (1938). *The five Chinese brothers*. New York: The Trumpet Club.

Bissex, G. L. (1980). *GNYS AT WRK: A child learns to write and read*. Cambridge, MA: Harvard University Press.

Boynton, S. (1995). *Blue hat, green hat*. New York: Simon & Schuster.

Braine, M.D.S. (1971). On two types of models of the internalization of grammars. In D. Slobin (Ed.), *The ontogenesis of grammar*. New York: Academic Press.

Brett, J. (1981). *Fritz and the beautiful horses*. Boston: Houghton Mifflin.

Brett, J. (1989). *Beauty and the beast*. New York: Scholastic.

Brett, J. (2005). *Honey . . . honey . . . lion!* New York: G. P. Putnam.

Bridwell, N. (1972). *Clifford the small red puppy*. New York: Scholastic.

Brown, M. (1947). *Goodnight, moon*. New York: HarperCollins.

Brumbeau, J. (2000). *The quilt maker's gift*. Duluth, MN: Pfeifer-Hamilton.

Bruner, J. (1981). The pragmatics of acquisition. In W. Deutsch (Ed.), *The child's construction of language*. New York: Academic Press.

Burningham, J. (1980). *The shopping basket*. Cambridge, MA: Candlewick Press.

Carle, E. (nd). *Have you seen my cat?* New York: Aladdin Paperbacks.

Carle, E. (1984). *The very busy spider*. New York: Philomel Books.

Carle, E. (1987). *The very hungry caterpillar*. New York: Philomel Books.

Carle, E. (1990). *The very quiet cricket*. New York: Philomel Books.

Carle, E. (1997). *From head to toe*. New York: Scholastic.

Carlson, N. (1990). *I like me!* New York: Puffin Books.

Carr, K. (2002). *Dinosaur hunt*. New York: HarperCollins.

Chodos-Irvine, M. (2003). *Ella Sarah gets dressed*. New York: Harcourt.

Chomsky, N. (2000). *New horizons in the study of language and mind*. New York: Cambridge University Press.

Christelow, E. (1989). *Five little monkeys jumping on the bed.* New York: Clarion Books.

Cole, B. (1987). *Prince Cinders.* New York: Putnam.

Conford, E. (1974). *Just the thing for Geraldine.* New York: Little, Brown.

Coville, B. (1979). *Sarah's unicorn.* New York: HarperCollins.

Curtis, J. L. (1998). *Today I feel silly and other moods that make my day.* New York: HarperCollins.

Curtis, J. L. (2002). *I'm gonna like me.* New York: HarperCollins.

DiCamillo, K. (2005). *Mercy Watson to the rescue.* Cambridge, MA: Candlewick Press.

Dodson, P. (1995). *An alphabet of dinosaurs.* New York: Scholastic.

Donaldson, M. (1979). *Children's minds.* New York: W. W. Norton & Company.

Dowson, N. (2004). *Tigress.* Cambridge, MA: Candlewick Press.

Dunrea, O. (2002). *Gossie.* Boston: Houghton Mifflin.

Dyson, A. H. (1989). *Multiple worlds of child writers: Friends learning to write.* New York: Teachers College Press.

Dyson, A. H. (1993). *Social worlds of children learning to write in an urban primary school.* New York: Teachers College Press.

Eimas, P. D., Sigueland, E. R., Jusczyk, P., & Vigorito, J. (1971). Speech perception in infants. *Science, 171,* 303–306.

Fillmore, L. W. (1976). *The second time around: Cognitive and social strategies in second language acquisition.* Doctoral dissertation. Stanford University, Stanford, CA.

Fox, M. (1988). *Koala Lou.* New York: Voyager Books.

Fox, M. (2004). *Where is the green sheep?* New York: Harcourt.

French, V. (2006). *T-Rex.* Cambridge, MA: Candlewick Press.

Ga'g, W. (1928/1996). *Millions of cats.* New York: Penguin Putnam Books.

Galdone, P. (1986). *Over in the meadow.* New York: Aladdin Paperbacks.

Graves, D. (1983). *Writing: Teachers and children at work.* Portsmouth, NH: Heinemann.

Gray, N. (1988). *A country far away.* New York: Orchard Books.

Gref, S. (2002). *Knock knock.* Orlando, FL: Harcourt, Inc.

Henkes, K. (1991). *Chrysanthemum.* New York: Scholastic.

Henkes, K. (1996). *Lilly's purple plastic purse.* New York: Greenwillow Books.

Hest, A. (1996). *Jamaica Louise James.* Cambridge, MA: Candlewick Press.

Hoffman, C., & Sharp, C. (1999). Children become writers: A conversation with two teachers. In J. Lindfors & J. Townsend (Eds.), *Teaching language arts: Learning through dialogue* (pp. 7–29). Urbana, IL: National Council of Teachers of English.

Hoffman, M. (1991). *Amazing Grace.* New York: Dial Books.

Holdaway, D. (1979). *The foundations of literacy.* Sydney, Australia: Ashton Scholastic.

Hollander, C. (2002). *A snack for Mack.* New York: Scholastic.

Holtz, L. T. (Ed.) (1995). *My first body book.* New York: Dorling Kindersley.

Hutchins, P. (1971). *Rosie's walk.* New York: Simon & Schuster.

Jackson, A. (1997). *I know an old lady who swallowed a pie.* New York: Puffin Books.

Langstaff, J. (1985). *Over in the meadow.* New York: Voyager Books.

Lester, H. (1988). *Tacky the penguin.* New York: Trumpet Club.

Lester, H. (1996). *Princess Penelope's parrot.* Boston: Houghton Mifflin.

Lester, H. (2003). *Something might happen.* Boston: Houghton Mifflin.

Lindfors, J. W. (1987). *Children's language and learning* (2nd ed). Englewood Cliffs, NJ: Prentice-Hall.

Lindfors, J. W., (1994). I hear voices. In A. D. Flurkey & R. J. Meyer (Eds.), *Under the whole language umbrella: Many cultures, many voices.* Urbana, IL: National Council of Teachers of English.

Lindfors, J. W., & Townsend, J. S. (1999). *Teaching language arts: Learning through dialogue.* Urbana, IL: National Council of Teachers of English.

Lionni, Leo (1964). *Tico and the golden wings.* New York: Alfred A. Knopf.

Lovell, P. (2001). *Stand tall, Molly Lou Melon.* New York: G. P. Putnam.

Marshall, J. (1987). *Red Riding Hood.* New York: Penguin Putnam.

Marshall, J. (1988). *Goldilocks and the three bears.* New York: Puffin Books.

Marshall, J. (1989). *The three little pigs.* New York: Puffin Books.

Martin, B., Jr. (1995). *Brown bear, brown bear, what do you see?* New York: Henry Holt.

Mayer, M. (1973). *Bubble, bubble.* New York: Parents' Magazine Press.

McNeill, D. (1966). Developmental psycholinguistics. In F. Smith & G. Miller (Eds.), *The genesis of language.* Cambridge, MA: MIT Press.

Munsch, R. (1980). *The paper bag princess.* New York: Annick Press.

Murawski, D. (2000). *Bug faces.* Washington, DC: National Geographic Society.

Nelson, K., & Gruendel, J. (1988). "At morning it's lunchtime": A scriptal view of children's dialogue. In M. Franklin & S. Barten (Eds.), *Child language: A reader.* New York: Oxford University Press.

Newkirk, T. (1984). Archimedes' dream. *Language Arts, 61,* 341–350.

Numeroff, L. (2004). *Beatrice doesn't want to.* Cambridge, MA: Candlewick Press.

O'Neill, A. (2002). *The recess queen.* New York: Scholastic.

Pilkey, D. (nd). *Captain Underpants* series. New York: Scholastic.

Pinkney, J. (1999). *The ugly duckling.* New York: Morrow Junior Books.

Polacco, P. (1999). *Luba and the wren.* New York: Philomel Books.

Rathman, P. (1996). *Officer Buckle and Gloria.* New York: Scholastic.

Rey, H. A., & Rey, M. (2001). Curious George goes to the hospital. In *The Complete adventures of Curious George.* Boston: Houghton Mifflin.

Roeper, T. (2006). *The prism of grammar: How child language illuminates humanism.* Cambridge, MA: MIT Press.

Root, P. (1998). *What baby wants.* Cambridge, MA: Candlewick Press.

Rosenblatt, L. (1978). *The reader, the text, the poem.* Carbondale: Southern Illinois Univeristy Press.

Sabuda, R., & Reinhart, M. (2005). *Encyclopedia prehistorica: Dinosaurs.* Cambridge, MA: Candlewick Press.

Schickedanz, J. A., & Sullivan, M. (1984, January). "Mom, What does U-F-F spell?" *Language arts, 61*(1), 7–17.

Schwartz, D. M. (1985). *How much is a million?* New York: Lothrop, Lee & Shepard Books.

Seuss, Dr. (1957). *The cat in the hat.* New York: Random House.

Shannon, D. (1998). *No, David!* New York: The Blue Sky Press.

Shannon, D. (1999). *David goes to school.* New York: The Blue Sky Press.

Sharratt, N. (2002). *Once upon a time.* Cambridge, MA: Candlewick Press.

Sharratt, N. (2003). *Ahoy, Pirate Pete!* Cambridge, MA: Candlewick Press.

Slobodkina, E. (1968). *Caps for sale.* New York: HarperCollins.

Smith, F. (1973). Twelve easy ways to make learning to read difficult* (*and one difficult way to make it easy). In *Psycholinguistics and reading.* New York: Holt, Rinehart and Winston.

Smith, F. (1985). *Reading without nonsense* (2nd ed.). New York: Teachers College Press.

Spier, P. (1980). *People.* New York: Doubleday.

Spinelli, E. (1991). *Reptiles.* Lincolnwood, IL: W. H. Smith.

Stonehouse, B. (1999). *Fighters.* New York: Tangerine Press.

Swope, S. (1989). *The Araboolies of Liberty Street.* New York: Farrar, Straus and Giroux.

Taback, S. (1997). *There was an old lady who swallowed a fly.* New York: Scholastic.

Tafuri, N. (2001). *Silly little goose!* New York: Scholastic.

Trevarthen, C. (1977). Descriptive analyses of infant communicative behaviour. In H. R. Schaffer (Ed.), *Studies in mother–infant interaction* (pp. 227–270). New York: Academic Press.

Trivizas, E. (1993). *The three little wolves and the big bad pig.* New York: Aladdin Paperbacks.

Van Laan, N. (1992). *Possum come a'knockin.* New York: Random House.

Voake, C. (1997). *Ginger.* Cambridge, MA: Candlewick Press.

Vygotsky, L. S. (1978). *Mind in society* (M. Cole, Ed.). Cambridge, MA: Harvard University Press.

Vygotsky, L. S. (1986). *Thought and language.* (A. Kozulin, Ed.). Cambridge, MA: MIT Press.

Waddell, M. (2003). *Hi, Harry!* Cambridge, MA: Candlewick Press.

Wahl, S. (1985). *I can count the petals of a flower.* Reston, VA: National Council of Teachers of Mathematics.

Wallace, K. (1993). *Think of an eel.* Cambridge, MA: Candlewick Press.

Ward, C. (1988). *Cookie's week.* New York: Scholastic.

Weeks, S. (n.d.). *Mrs. McNosh hangs up her wash.* New York: HarperCollins.

White, E. B. (1952). *Charlotte's web.* New York: Harper & Row.

Willems, M. (2003). *Don't let the pigeon drive the bus.* New York: Hyperion Books for Children.

Willems, M. (2004). *Knuffle Bunny.* New York: Hyperion Books for Children.

Willems, M. (2007). *There is a bird on your head!* New York: Hyperion Books for Children.

Williams, L. (1986). *The little old lady who was not afraid of anything.* New York: Trumpet Club.

Williams, S. (1989). *I went walking.* New York: Voyager Books.

Williams, S. (2001). *Dinnertime!* New York: Harcourt.

Wilson, K. J. (2006). *When violence begins at home: A comprehensive guide to understanding and ending domestic abuse* (2nd ed.). Alameda, CA: Hunter House Publishers.

Wood, A., & Wood, D. (1984). *The napping house.* New York: Harcourt Brace.

Zemach, M. (1976). *It could always be worse.* New York: Farrar, Straus and Giroux.

Ziefert, H., & Taback, S. (1996). *Two little witches: A counting story.* Cambridge, MA: Candlewick Press.

Zion, G. (1956). *Harry the dirty dog.* New York: Trumpet Club.

Index

About the Author

Judith Wells Lindfors has been a teacher of second graders (in suburban Boston and Chicago), secondary school students (in Kisii, Kenya), and adults (in Los Angeles). She was a professor in the Department of Curriculum and Instruction (Language and Literacy) at The University of Texas at Austin from 1973 to 2000.

Her publications include *Children's Inquiry: Using Language to Make Sense of the World* and *Children's Language and Learning*, which won the Mina Shaughnessy Medal (Modern Language Association). Since 2001 she has been working as a volunteer at the charter school at SafePlace, Austin's domestic violence and sexual assault survival center.